Searching for the April Moon

NANCY ROBERTSON

Smithers BC Canada
2008

Creekstone Press, 7456 Driftwood Road
Smithers BC V0J 2N7 Canada
www.creekstonepress.com

Library and Archives Canada Cataloguing in Publication

Robertson, Nancy, 1944-
Searching for the April Moon / Nancy Robertson
ISBN 978-0-9783195-1-9
1. Robertson, Nancy, 1944- –Family. 2. Robertson, Nancy, 1944- –Travel.
3. Prince Rupert (B.C.) –Biography. 4. Nelson (B.C.) –Biography.
I. Title.
FC3849.P72Z48 2008   971.1'1   C2008-904107-0

Book Design: Hans Saefkow, Sheila Peters, and ArcheType Enterprises
Cover Design: Hans Saefkow

"Send flowers to the nurses" was first published in the anthology *Gifts of our
Fathers* (The Crossing Press, 1994). "Thursday afternoon" was first published
in the anthology *Looking Back, Stories of our Mothers & Fathers in Retrospect*
(New Brighton Books, 2003).

Nancy's brother Gerry bought her a camera when she was in her
early teens. Most of the photographs in the book are hers. The
others come from her family collection. The back cover photo
of Nancy is taken by her granddaughter, Allison Carelse.

Searching for the April Moon is typeset in Palatino and printed and
bound by Houghton Boston in Canada on Enviro 100 paper made
of 100% post-consumer waste and processed chlorine free.

Contents

Family Tree

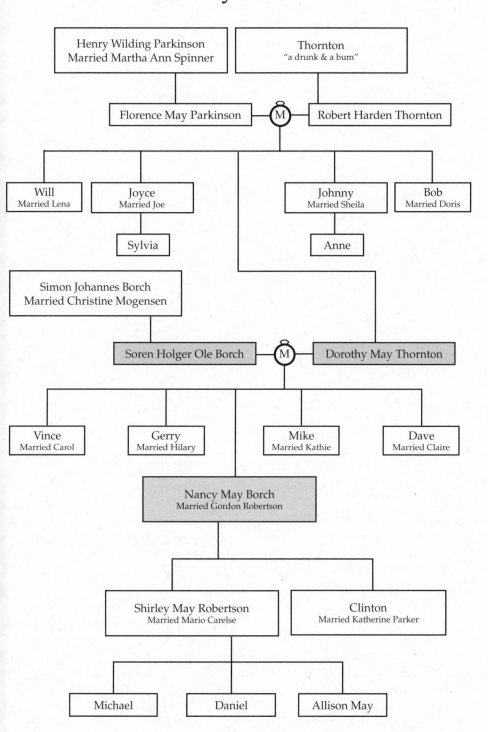

Henry Wilding Parkinson
Married Martha Ann Spinner

Thornton
"a drunk & a bum"

Florence May Parkinson — M — Robert Harden Thornton

Will
Married Lena

Joyce
Married Joe

Johnny
Married Sheila

Bob
Married Doris

Sylvia

Anne

Simon Johannes Borch
Married Christine Mogensen

Soren Holger Ole Borch — M — Dorothy May Thornton

Vince
Married Carol

Gerry
Married Hilary

Mike
Married Kathie

Dave
Married Claire

Nancy May Borch
Married Gordon Robertson

Shirley May Robertson
Married Mario Carelse

Clinton
Married Katherine Parker

Michael

Daniel

Allison May

Send flowers
to the nurses

*T*hose damn nurses aren't going to make me do what I don't want to. They're not going to get away with this. God damn."

Dad struggles against the restraint that holds him in bed. He throws aside the blankets. "God damn, let me out of here. Bring me my clothes. I'm going home."

"You can't, dear," says Mom.

"Damn you, you're on their side. You don't want me at home. Go to hell then."

"There's no need for that kind of talk," she says.

"I'll talk any God damn way I want to."

Why are you swearing? You didn't swear when we spilled our milk, broke the best china, chipped the ivory piano keys with the pliers. Now you're like a frightened bird, caught in the house, smashing from window to window.

—

Dad is in his wheelchair when I arrive at the hospital the next day. His meal tray is still in front of him. He is alone in the room. The other men eat their meals together in the lounge. Dad will not join them.

"Oh, good," I say as I bend over to kiss him. "You had strawberries for lunch."

"Yes, but they're sure tight on the good food."

"I'll bring you a clean housecoat tomorrow."

"Don't worry about it."

No, I won't worry about it and you won't worry about it. You will just be an old man sitting in a wheelchair, tied in so you can't fall and hurt yourself, dozing most of the day with your chin resting on the strawberry stains that alarm visitors to the ward. They don't know anything about you. They look at you with curiosity or fear and quickly look away. They don't know that your appearance was always impeccable, that you went on a picnic with white shirt and tie, that Mom took along a tablecloth, glass plates and silverware just for you. She took a cushion for you to sit on so you wouldn't get your suit pants dirty. She wore her oldest made-over clothes, her gardening shoes and lopsided hat. She picked berries or looked for pussy willows while you sat and read the paper.

You were always immaculate and tidy. Your hair never grew over your ears, your whiskers never left a shadow on your face, your pens and pencils were placed neatly on your smoking stand beside your chair in the living room. You used ironed cloth handkerchiefs, wore polished leather shoes, drove a washed and waxed car.

Now you sit, old and frail, stained and whiskered. I try not to ask, "How are you?" because sometimes you tell me. Then I don't know what to say. I hold your hand or rub your arm. I wish I hadn't asked.

I was seven when my tonsils were removed. You took me to the hospital on your way to work. You picked me up after work. You held my hand and asked me if I wanted to go home the high road or the low road. But my throat hurt too much to sing with you.

—

It's 3:30 before I get to the hospital. I sit with Dad for an hour. He's good today. He reads Maclean's. I look through the Daily News. I search the news, the editorials, the want ads and horoscopes. I don't know what I'm looking for and I don't find a new dimension or direction. No light turned on in a dark room.

I don't think Dad finds any illumination in Maclean's, either. He's too tired to look. He doesn't even talk about going home. He asks me to check to see if Mom has signed her will. He tells me his papers are in order, the house is paid for, he's left lots of money for Mom, and when she goes, it comes to us five kids.

"We don't care about the money, Dad."

"Yes," he says, "but I do."

You always cared about money. I was the youngest child and the only girl. You sat on the edge of my bed when you came to say goodnight, and told me that when you won the Irish Sweepstakes, you were taking Mom and me on a trip to Denmark. When I was older, you took me to the horse races and bet on all the long shots. But with my four brothers you set the example. You went to work every day and came home for supper on time. On paydays you counted the money by tens onto the kitchen table for Mom. She was responsible for the housekeeping on whatever amount you gave her. You looked after the finances. You paid the bills. When your sons grew up you were so proud of them. Their success was your success. You wore their promotions and accomplishments with shoulders back and chin up.

—

I take Mom to see Dad. He says everything hurts. His hands, feet, legs, back. He's confused. He doesn't know where he is. We wheel him out of his room, down the hallway, into the lounge so he can watch TV.

"You've done a good job of redecorating the living room, dear."

She's annoyed that he doesn't recognize where he is. She argues, "You're not at home."

He smiles sweetly. "I'm not going to bed early tonight. I'm going to wait and go to bed with you."

That night he fights the nurses. "Leave me alone, God damn it. Don't touch me. I'm waiting for Mom." He struggles so hard he tips the wheelchair over.

When I see him the next day he is tied into bed and the bars are up. A bandage rings his head. "I feel like such a damn nuisance."

"It's O.K., Dad."

"I'm ready to go," he says. "I'm ready. Everything is looked after." His chin quivers. "You take care of Mom. Make sure she gets my Canada Pension."

"I will, Dad."

"I know you will. And the supplement. Don't forget the supplement."

"I won't forget. I think I'll phone the boys tonight."

"No," he says, "let them phone you."

"But they don't know."

"Yes, they know. They will come when it's too late." He tells me to go home. "Your life is with Bill. Don't feel bad about me. Mom and I have had fifty-seven years together."

I don't want to leave. You saw me through some hard times. You travelled a thousand miles by Greyhound to be with me when I went to court for my divorce. You were not judgmental, you were just there. We drove that thousand miles back together in my blue Pontiac with my two children. You gave me a home until I found an apartment and a job. You took your grandson to nursery school and picked him up two hours later. You took both children to swimming lessons every Friday. You drew and painted with them at the kitchen table and taught them how to play checkers and gin rummy.

—

I take the clippers, scissors and comb with me today. I wheel him into the middle of the room. "Thanks," he says, "I need a trim."

I place the old sheet over his head, the sheet with the hole cut out of the centre. As I cut his hair, the other old men on the ward join us in their wheelchairs. We form a circle. My hands are the only movement, the scissors the only noise. When I finish Dad's haircut, I ask, "Anyone else?"

"Me," says one old man.

I take the sheet off Dad's shoulders and place it over the man's head.

"No," says Dad. "You came to see me."

"I know, Dad, but this won't take long."

"I won't have it. Get me away from here."

I wheel him back beside his bed. "I won't be long," I say.

He often complains about the other men. Says how rude and noisy they are. The man across the room beats the wall with his cane when he needs a nurse instead of ringing the call bell clipped to his sheet.

You were always decent, but you were never a prude. You took my youngest brother, Dave, and me to our first evening movie, *Picnic*. William Holden and Kim Novak. I was about nine or ten. It didn't take you long to realize the subject matter wasn't the same as a Saturday afternoon matinee. You stood and told us we were leaving, but Dave and I pleaded with you. You sat back down and watched the movie with us.

—

My eldest brother phones. "I'm arriving on the evening flight. How's Dad?"

"Not very good. I'm glad you're coming. I'll pick you up at the airport."

I visit Dad in the afternoon. A nurse is setting up the oxygen. She arranges tubes around his head. "He's not with us today," she says.

I lean over the bars and kiss him on the cheek. "Hi, Dad."

His eyes focus on my face. He smiles and says, "Hi, honey."

I tell him the news of the visit. "I'll bring Vince to see you as soon as he arrives."

"He's already been here. He came this morning."

"I don't think so, Dad. His plane arrives after supper. I told him I'd pick him up."

"He's already been here. He was here the same time as Brian Mulroney and Vander Zalm. Mulroney and Vander Zalm were drunk as lords."

Dad has never liked Brian Mulroney and he has been mad at Vander Zalm for years. "We need more men like Trudeau," he'd tell me whenever we discussed politics.

Mom is going to be mad at Dad. "Don't talk silly," she'll say. But I sit and agree with him as he rambles on about his world as he sees it today.

I feel badly my brother is going to see you like this. You were always stable, sensible, sober. You weren't a drinking man. When my brother, Gerry, returned from his trip to Europe with a bottle of champagne from France, Mom brought out the Danish crystal and placed nine glasses around the dining room table that was set with one of your mother's finest Danish linens. My grandparents, Mom's parents, were also there for supper. We all sat around the table and watched you cut the roast paper-thin. The plates were stacked in front of you and you dished up the meat for each of us. When we were all served, you opened and poured the champagne. Dave and I were given the same as the others even though we were barely teenagers. You raised your glass and gave a toast in celebration of your son's return.

—

At the airport I suggest to Vince that we go for a beer. I want to cushion the news about Dad. When we get to the hospital Mom is already there. "I don't know what's the matter with him," she says. "He's not himself." She looks scared, not mad.

I lean over and take Dad's hand. I give his shoulder a little shake. "Hi, Dad. Look who's come to see you." I point to the other side of the bed. His eyes follow mine.

"Hello, Dad," my brother says. "How are you?"

"I'm fine, Vince," he answers groggily. "How good of you to come and see me. How's the family?"

"Everyone's fine. They send their love."

"You tell them I love them." He closes his eyes. After a while we hear a light snore. Vince doesn't want to leave him. He thinks he might go at any time.

When I was a young girl you took me to the café every Sunday. You told me I could have either a comic book or a chocolate bar. I sat on the floor looking through my favourite comics, then through the glass cabinet that held the sweets, and agonized over my choice. You never rushed my decision. You sat on a stool and had a cup of coffee and a smoke.

—

I hear his hollering as I step off the elevator. "Mom! MOM! M-O-O-O-M! Come here! Where the hell are you? Come here right now!" As I enter the room he asks, "Where's Mom? Everyone's waiting. See? There's Mike and Kathie. Oh, look! Melissa and Shelley are with them."

His face is flushed, his eyes bright. His smile crinkles his eyes, his heels shuffle back and forth under the sheet. His arm reaches towards the ceiling and he shakes his son's hand. He walks to Kathie and extends his hand. "How wonderful to see you."

He greets them all, every member of his family including the latest great grandchild. He remembers every name as they appear for him on the ceiling of his hospital room. He moves his legs as he crosses streets, goes down sidewalks. He shakes hands, admires new homes, teases the youngsters.

He is so busy he doesn't notice Mom arrive. She doesn't stay. She can't bear to see him like this. "He has always been a gentleman," she says. "He would never make a scene. He would never raise his voice. I don't want to remember him this way."

I stay with him until he settles back in bed.

"Did you have a good time?" he asks.

"Yes," I say. "Did you?"

"I had a wonderful time."

You always enjoyed family. You and Mom travelled every September to visit each of us. You welcomed in-laws and grandchildren without reservation. Mom suggested going to the Queen Charlotte Islands or taking an Alaskan cruise but you just wanted to visit your adult children. You said you were a lucky man to have such a family.

—

I sit on the chair beside Dad's bed. My arms lean on the bars that hold him in like a crib. I rest my head on my arms. It's been a long day. I don't think he knows I'm here but I don't want to leave him. The only noise in the room is the sputtering from the oxygen on the wall. The tube drapes gracefully from the wall to the bed where it rests along the sheets, pillow and finally Dad's head where it looks like he's wearing a headset for listening to music, except the small plugs are in his nose, not his ears. He is not fighting, not even with the intravenous needle taped to the top of his hand.

I'm scared to touch him in case I hurt him. His thin arms lie outside the sheets, his elbows and fingers bumpy and twisted from the arthritis that has plagued him for years.

I have to go to the bathroom. I'm hungry. I'm stiff from sitting so long. I'm tired. Yet something keeps me here, searching his face. I'm sitting here like an outsider when inside I'm standing on tiptoes, peeking over, trying to see something. I know if I leave, I may not find it.

He opens his eyes. His hand trembles as he attempts to lift it from the sheet. I reach between the bars and hold his hand, gently. The skin feels like tissue paper but there is pressure from his fingers as he turns his hand, palm to palm, with mine.

"I love you, Dad."

"I know," he says. "I love you, too, honey." His words are slow, his voice weak. "Telegraph the boys and please send flowers to the nurses." His eyes close, his hand relaxes. His life is over. One tear escapes and slowly slips down his cheek.

I sit with my hand in his until I can't stand the stiffness in my arms and back any longer. The chair is hard and the position awkward. My arms and shoulders hurt where the metal bars press into me. I have to go to the bathroom. I can't wait any longer. I use the one in Dad's room and hope that no one comes in.

I walk to the nursing station. Then I walk home. Rain runs off my hat, down my cheeks, drips from my chin and soaks my collar. Dampness spreads to my shoulders. Wet pants cling to my thighs.

I have a hot bath when I get home. My legs are cold and red and sting when they hit the hot water. I lie back in the tub and hold up my hands. The skin is slack with lines at the wrists and tiny wrinkles like cross-stitch across the front.

I think of him, how he polished our shoes every Saturday night, taught us to play ping-pong, and how he could add columns of figures in his head and get the correct answer while we were still adding one column at a time, carrying forward to the next row. I think of him, when he came home from work, how he would sneak up behind Mom, put his arms around her waist and give her a smooch on the back of her neck.

"No, dear, not now," she complained as she stirred the gravy or salted the potatoes. He turned and winked at us kids.

The phone rings. It stops after the sixth ring. I climb out of the tub, dry myself and put on a warm housecoat. "Better get busy," I think.

He would expect me to do things right.

Trying to sing my own song

I am having trouble sorting out the difference between kindness and stupidity. My neighbour, who knows Bill and I go away every winter, phoned to ask if I would like to have a housesitter instead of leaving our home empty for several months. She told me there's a woman who lives on a boat who would like a house to live in for the winter. The woman has a five-year-old son. Last year she became romantically involved with a married man. He left his wife and family and moved into a cabin on a lake just outside of town with this woman. Recently she decided she would rather be on her own.

"He has problems," my neighbour said.

The man decided it was all too much for him. He did not succeed in his attempt to end his life, but is still in the hospital. His girlfriend moved from his cabin on the lake to his sailboat in the harbour.

Soon he will be released. She cannot continue living on his sailboat unless she wants to resume the affair. Counselors have suggested they work on their relationship gradually, without living together. But monetary matters have put her in a dilemma. She cannot afford to rent a place right now. My neighbour suggested to her friend that she housesit until she gets back on her feet financially.

At least my neighbour was honest with me. She actually told me all this. Maybe it would have been better if she had just phoned and asked if I wanted a friend of hers to housesit. I might have mulled it over, then said, "What the hell, probably a good idea to have someone in the house." Instead she told me about her friend's problems and the boyfriend who tried to commit suicide.

I'd rather not have young children in the house but it was the boyfriend who worried me. I could envision his brains all over my living room. His blood on my walls.

So instead of telling my neighbour my fears, and risking looking unkind, I used Mom for an excuse. "My mother hasn't been very well this fall so I'm not sure when we are leaving."

Mom has never held me back. She has always encouraged me to travel. "I wish I'd had your opportunities when I was young," she said when I was eighteen and we were packing a trunk for my move to Whitehorse. I know Mom worried about me. Not that she said anything but I know how I felt when my daughter left home after high school. I missed her terribly and prayed that nothing would harm her.

But mingled with my fear and loneliness was a fierce pride that she wanted to experience life on her own terms.

Now Mom says to me, "You go while you still can. Don't worry about me."

Each year it becomes more difficult to leave her. But I want to go. I'm not getting any younger. I only have one life. Excuses to justify travel and adventure over the anxiety and guilt of leaving Mom alone.

Saying goodbye is a moment so painful we do not say the words out loud anymore. She pushes her wheelchair through her congested living room to the doorway so she can wave goodbye. Furniture and doorways are scraped and bashed by the wheelchair. Knick-knacks, vases, plants and pictures adorn window ledges, bookcases, coffee table and TV. Paintings, photos, cards and calendars crowd walls. Her belongings frame her in her wheelchair in the doorway. Her body is humped over. Her left hand wraps her crippled right fingers around the bar bolted to the doorjamb. She struggles to get up from her wheelchair. When she gets to her feet she grabs her four-pronged cane with her left hand. She doesn't stand tall anymore but lifts her white-capped head to see me. Her face is scrunched up and her lips tremble. Tears escape and trickle down her cheeks. After a kiss and a long hug, I cannot look at her. I close the front door behind me. I wave to her like I always do, from the sidewalk along Ninth Avenue. For this goodbye I cannot see if she is waving back.

But even if I knew when I was leaving, I'm not sure I would have told my neighbour. I didn't want her friend to housesit. Why didn't I tell the truth? I have no problem being honest with Mom. Not any more. For years I found her impatient and critical and I avoided her. I had excuses ready to refuse the weekly invitations to Sunday dinner. But I couldn't avoid occasions like birthdays and holidays. I was bombarded with questions about my choices in life. "When are you going to settle down again? Why don't you get married?" She questioned my methods of raising my children. "You spoil those two kids. Where are they? Why aren't they here?" She complained about Dad. "He won't go anywhere or do anything. He just sits in front of that blaring TV all day."

When Dad was no longer able to drive his car, I took Mom grocery shopping every Thursday evening. I dreaded her comments and questions. "You're quiet tonight. How come you're always so quiet?"

"I'm tired."

"How come you're so tired?"

"I had a busy day at work."

"You're a young woman yet. That shouldn't bother you."

"I didn't sleep well last night."

"Why? What's the matter with you?"

"Nothing, Mom. Nothing's the matter."

"There must be something the matter. You're always tired. Are you sick?"

"No, Mom, I'm fine."

"So why are you so quiet?"

Silence. My defense. I was the closest one for her to swing at. Silence was the only way I could swing back.

When we got to Overwaitea, my impatience surfaced and I tried to hurry her through the aisles. But this was her escape from the house and the responsibilities of caring for her cranky old husband and she would not be hurried. This was a social event. She stopped to talk to music pupils, church friends, neighbours. She read packaging, compared prices, checked new products. But when we reached the checkout, she got impatient with any delay. "What's the matter now? Where do they find these girls? Don't they know anything anymore?"

I pretended I wasn't with her, that I didn't know her. She continued asking questions but I ignored her.

She complained if she wasn't invited out but criticized any drinking of alcohol if she was. I didn't tell her about my private life – the parties, the drinking. She demanded perfection from everyone and was vocal in her disappointment when her level wasn't met. I didn't like her much for years, but it wasn't until after Dad died, and after a massive stroke crippled her two months later, that I saw how lost and alone she was. When I drove her home from the hospital six months after her stroke she sat in Dad's chair and wept. I didn't want to leave her. But I didn't want to stay, either. I was on a teeter-totter with concern for her on one end, and the inconvenience to me on the other. Then something happened that forced me to attempt honesty with my mother.

Out-of-town friends visited on a sunny summer Sunday. We phoned local friends and soon a party was underway on our backyard patio. Families arrived with young children and grandparents. Everyone brought food or alcohol or both. Some people drank and some didn't. I did. Soon I was somersaulting down the lawn with the children. I was enjoying myself until one woman asked, "Where's your mom?"

"It's too difficult to get her to the backyard in a wheelchair."

"There are enough people to help," she insisted.

I ignored her. I didn't want Mom at the party. I knew I wouldn't be able to drink and somersault in front of her.

I felt uneasy with my excuse and slept restlessly that night. The next day I walked to Mom's home. I told her that we had had a party and the reason I hadn't invited her was because I knew she didn't like being around people who were drinking and I was drinking yesterday. I was totally honest with her about my feelings of discomfort and how I believed I would have to behave if she was there.

Mom sat in her wheelchair, stared into her lap and twisted one of Dad's old cotton handkerchiefs between her fingers. Finally she shook the handkerchief loose and blew her nose. She said, "Mealtimes are the worst. I hate eating alone." I reached over and took one of her hands in mine. "The nights," she said, "the nights are so long. You lie beside a man for fifty-seven years and when he goes, the bed is awfully lonely."

She wiped her eyes with her free hand. She lifted her head, looked me directly in the eyes and said, "I guess I'm going to have to learn to adjust if I want to be invited."

I was forty-six and she was almost eighty-one. Talk about adjustments. I love being myself around Mom and I love liking her. She is cheerful and relaxed and enjoys being included. She drinks a glass of wine when she comes for Sunday supper. Our family cannot believe the change. She is teased by her grandchildren and jokes with her in-laws.

I am lucky to have Mom with me. We got it right. Our time together is valuable. I enjoy most of the time I spend with her. I look forward to our daily walk up and down her wheelchair ramp, our weekly game of Scrabble, a drive on a sunny day and stopping at McDonald's for ice cream. Sometimes the amount of time involved frustrates me. Soaking infected toenails in Epsom salts, unexpected shopping trips for personal items, feeling responsible for her well-being. The list of things-to-do for Mom never ends.

Aspects of her life must be equally frustrating. She cannot go by herself to buy new stockings or satisfy an unexpected chocolate urge. She cannot tend her garden or walk to the corner store for the Sunday Province.

And every year, as she gets frailer, my own time shrinks.

After my neighbour's phone call I moved the fridge and freezer into the middle of the kitchen floor and swept the cobwebs and dust that had collected since last fall. I got down on my hands and knees and scrubbed the floor, the back of the freezer and the top and sides of the fridge. I vacuumed the dust from the screen on the back of the fridge. I wiped the dust from the cord that slung from the fridge to the plug-in.

While I waited for the floor to dry behind the fridge and freezer, I phoned my daughter long-distance. She wasn't home and I didn't want to tell her answering machine to put me in a home when I couldn't care for myself anymore, so I hung up.

I don't think I listen to anything except the tune in my own head. I don't always hear what others say to me. I make up my own words for songs. For the longest time, I sang, "Hey, Love, got me on my knees. Hey, Love, got me begging please." When my son told me the word in the Eric Clapton song was "Layla" not "Hey, Love" I argued with him. I didn't want to change the lyrics. It wrecked the song for me. Whenever I hear it now I sing "Hey, Love" but it's not the same. The real words have crept into my mind and spoiled the image.

As I scrubbed the floor I thought about my response to my neighbour. I used Mom for an excuse rather than make a decision. Mom would not worry about it one way or the other. I was not concerned about her reaction. And I have family and friends who would have told me that someone else's problems were not mine and that letting out my house would be sheer stupidity. So why was I phoning my daughter to advise her about my old age? Maybe if I had talked to her, I would have phoned my neighbour and said, "Wait a minute. Let me think this over."

I was phoning my daughter because my lack of compassion for another woman upset me. I started reading feminist magazines and books in the mid-eighties, the same time as my daughter was a university student taking Women's Studies classes. She was a radical feminist and I was a closet feminist. Although we agreed in principle, our approach was different. She worked the crisis line for Women Against Violence Against Women and I wrote poetry. She voiced out loud her dislike of a rape joke at a family gathering while I just didn't laugh at the joke. She confronted issues and ruffled feathers. I read more books and started writing stories that I didn't want anyone I knew to read.

We talked and argued and cried and laughed and hugged our way through the eighties. It was painful for me to be confronted by my daughter when I wanted to avoid subjects like child or sexual abuse. I wanted to be perfect for her. I wanted her to like me.

Here was my chance to show her that all those struggles together had left me a more compassionate and understanding woman. Instead I discovered that my possessions and privacy were more important to me than helping or caring for another human being. I knew so little about suicide that I feared the suicidal. I was embarrassed I did not have a kind or humane reaction to someone with emotional problems.

Maybe my reaction was based on my own failed marriage of many years ago. From the violence that erupted when I left him. His smashing down locked doors. His threats. His promise to take me with him when he left this world.

My reaction wasn't based on concern for the safety and comfort of a woman with a child who needed a place to live. I could have extended a helping hand. I've been on that road. Two young children. Broke. No place to live. An explosive relationship.

I do not want these complications back in my life in any form.

So why am I uncomfortable with my decision? It's like someone just told me the real words and spoiled the way I was singing my song.

Searching for the April moon

I heard on the radio that the reason the moon looks so big in April is because it is ten times closer to the earth in April than at any other time of year. I checked the calendar and found there were four days until the full moon. That evening I went outside, stood on the back deck and searched the sky for the April moon. The night was black and a drizzle of rain misted my face.

It rained all the next day. Several times during the evening I pulled the curtains aside on the back porch and looked out. It was still raining. The third night, wind smashed raindrops against the back window.

The next evening, according to my calendar and the radio, the full moon should have been right over my back yard. I put on my oilskins, stepped into my gumboots, and went outside. Wind whipped my body and rain lashed my face.

The storm let up the next day but the sky was still gray. For another week I continued to go outside several times each evening, later and later, hoping to see the moon rise over the mountain. But clouds hung low and spoiled my search.

"Damn," I said as I slammed the back door shut.

Bill looked up from his Princess Auto catalogue. "What's the matter?"

"Everything's the matter and I'm sick of this lousy weather."

He put a marker in the catalogue and set it on the coffee table. "What's really bugging you?" he asked.

"The weather. I wanted to see the full moon this month and now it's too late. It's over. You'd think those clouds could have lifted just one night."

"I'm sure there will be another full moon in your lifetime."

"I wanted to see the April moon," I stressed.

"Why? What's so important about the April moon?"

"The moon is ten times closer to the earth in April."

"Impossible," he said. "Absolutely impossible."

"Well, that's what I heard on the radio."

"Maybe you did but I know the moon couldn't be ten times closer to the earth at any time. It could be ten percent closer but not ten times closer. And it doesn't have to be April to be closest to the earth."

"That's what I heard," I grumbled as I walked over to the bookshelf and removed Volume 15 of the encyclopedia: MEX to NAT.

"*Moon*, natural satellite of a planet, in particular, the single natural satellite of the earth. The moon is the earth's nearest neighbour in space. Man has studied the moon since the beginning of time and recorded its apparent motions through the sky. The study of the moon in earnest began with the invention of the telescope by Galileo in 1610 and culminated in 1969 when man first actually set foot on the moon's surface."

I scanned the pages. "At perigee, when the moon is nearest the earth, the distance is about 227,000 mi (365,000 km); at apogee, when the moon is farthest from the earth, the distance is about 254,000 mi (409,000 km). The average distance is about 240,000 mi (385,000 km)."

I should have known there was no sense doubting Bill about anything scientific, mechanical or practical. He understands how and why things work. Right now he has his eye on Mom's grandfather clock. It's getting old and temperamental. "Like me," says Mom. "It doesn't work properly anymore, either."

The clock chimed the hour, on the hour, for sixty years. Lately it loses time or stops. The only way to get it started is to tilt it on its side several times. During the day, Mom struggles out of her chair and into her wheelchair just to adjust the clock. "That darn clock. What's the matter with it?"

Bill checked with jewelers but they said there was no one in town who repairs clocks. Someday, when it stops for good, Bill will take it apart. I'll bet money he'll fix it.

"What's really the matter, Nancy?" he asked. "Is it your mother?"

I felt the sting in the back of my eyes.

"Is she all right?"

I nodded. "I cut her toenails this morning and I accidentally cut one of her toes. It wouldn't stop bleeding. I've been back and forth today like a yo-yo. I had to keep changing the bandage."

He knew I hated cutting Mom's toenails. I couldn't stand the smell. The first time I cut them she sat in her wheelchair and I sat on the floor. I was lightheaded when I finished. I could barely walk to her bathroom to scrub my hands. I left immediately. "I have to go, Mom. Goodbye."

—

One winter, when Bill and I had camped on Shipwreck Beach on the southern tip of the Baja peninsula, a black truck with a small black camper perched on the back drove off the dirt road into the desert and stopped about a hundred feet from us. A man limped up to our campsite. "Excuse me," he said, "I hate to ask, but would you please help me."

"What can I do?" Bill asked.

"I need you to take some cactus out of my foot."

The man told us he had walked into a cactus and the needles in between his toes and on the bottom of his foot had broken off and his foot was infected.

Bill sat in a lawn chair and the man sat on our indoor-outdoor carpet with his foot on Bill's lap. He never flinched or moved his foot while Bill dug in, sometimes a quarter of an inch, to remove the needles.

While Bill extracted needles, the man talked. He told us he had worked for NASA in the sixties. His job was to put a man on the moon. He was one of forty computer programmers who worked endless hours to ensure that the lunar module successfully left the spacecraft, landed on the moon, blasted off from the moon and rejoined the command ship.

On July 20, 1969, he watched Neil Armstrong and Buzz Aldrin step out onto the moon. He never stopped watching until the lunar module returned safely to the command ship. Then he went out and got drunk. He drank for three days not knowing if the three astronauts arrived safely back on earth.

After the third day, he went to work and quit his job. "What took you so long?" asked his boss. "You're number twenty-seven." All forty programmers quit their jobs.

—

I bent over and ran my hand over Dad's headstone. I brushed long, dead grass aside and pulled wet moss from the edges. I knew Mom was watching from the car. She would have done this herself if she could. But it was too far for her to walk and too far for her to bend over and tidy the stone.

Dad is on the high side of the cemetery. That pleased Mom. "Good drainage," she said. "I'm glad he has good drainage."

A full season had passed since we were here last. Old grass entwined new growth over the edges of the stone. Some of the grass stuck and my hand rubbed to remove it. My fingers picked out the stubborn pieces caught in his surname, BORCH. There wasn't enough room on the stone for all Dad's given names, Soren Holger Ole Gylding, so she decided to use his initials, along with the name he was called, Ole. So carved into the stone, under BORCH, is:

1906 S.H.Ole G. 1989

My eye always sees S.H.O.G., which makes no sense to me. I have to remind myself of the process Mom went through to arrive at this lettering. She wanted all his names recognized.

There is enough space for all the letters of Mom's name on the stone. She made me promise to remember to have both her names, Dorothy May, engraved under Dad's, and the dates, when the time came.

Mom watched me walk back to the car. She reached for my hand after I got in.

"Is everything all right?" she asked. "Isn't the city keeping the grass cut?"

"Everything's fine, Mom."

"What took you so long?"

"I pulled the moss out and cleared off the old grass."

"Oh, thank you. Thank you," she said.

—

On one of our trips down Baja, Bill and I had driven to an isolated area about half way down the Sea of Cortez side of the peninsula. We pulled off the road and stopped at a lovely spot overlooking the ocean and a white sandy bay. We stopped for lunch and stayed the winter.

One day, when we were riding our bikes, we met two kayakers camped in a cove. It was a treat for us to speak English to someone aside from each other. When they offered us a beer we didn't refuse.

Don told us that his father had recently retired. He had just bought a new motorhome to travel down Baja when he suffered a massive heart attack and died. Don's eyes filled with tears. "He would have loved camping here." He reached into his cooler for more beer.

"No more for us, Don," Bill said. "We better go."

"Please stay. Just one more."

Bill looked at his watch.

"Let's have one more," I said remembering the previous winter when I had spent many nights in front of a campfire grieving the loss of Dad.

We finished our beer while dusk settled in, said our good-byes and rode our bikes back to the main dirt road. Within minutes it was totally dark. Clouds had moved in during the afternoon and blackened any light from the sky. There was no moon to guide us home. We could see nothing. Not the road. Not each other.

We walked with our bicycles on the outside of the narrow road. We hung onto our bikes as they dropped off the road or dipped in and out of ditches. After walking about an hour we thought we should be close to the trail that would take us to our campsite. We stopped often, searching the sky, wishing for the moon. But absolute darkness enveloped us.

My bike scraped against a rock cliff. "We've gone too far."

"How do you know?" Bill asked.

"This is where we met the bulls the other day."

We had been riding home from a soak in natural hot springs when we met a dozen Brahman bulls on this part of the narrow road. We stopped and got off our bikes.

"Aren't these the dangerous bulls they ride in rodeos?" Bill had asked when he saw the size of the animals and the hump over their shoulders.

"They won't hurt us," I said.

"How do you know?"

"They're just grazing. There's no bucking strap tied around their flank like at rodeos and they haven't just been hit with electric prods or spurs." I pushed my bike towards the bulls. They sauntered along and clambered off the road as the cliffs rounded back into the desert. Bill waited until the road was clear then we rode our bikes the short distance home.

I had placed a large white rock at the entrance to our trail shortly after we'd arrived. So we turned around that black night and searched until we found that rock.

―

I walked over to Mom's house to take her for her daily walk. She asked if I would be going downtown, and if so, would I be going to the bank.

"If you need something, I'll go," I said.

"I need some money."

"O.K. Write me a cheque and I'll cash it."

She maneuvered her wheelchair into the bedroom and got her purse from its hiding place. She worked her way back into the living room.

"Who do I make it out to?" she asked.

"To me," I said.

"Who are you?"

"Nancy Robertson," I answered.

"Oh, right," she said.

I took the money to Mom the next day. Then I took her for her walk, up and down the wheelchair ramp, three times. "Gerry will be here next week," I said as I walked the well-worn path beside the ramp. My brother, Gerry, and his wife, Hilary, came every September to visit Mom.

"He's not coming to see me," she said.

"Yes, he is."

"No, he's not. He's coming to see that other woman."

"What other woman?"

"You know. That OTHER woman."

"There's only you and me here, Mom."

"His daughter. He's coming to see his daughter."

"She doesn't live here."

"No. Dad's coming. Dad's coming to see his daughter."

"It's me, Mom. It's me, Nancy. Gerry is coming to see you and me. I'm his sister."

She stopped and looked down at me from the ramp. "Nancy? Of course. What's the matter with me, anyway?"

The next day I walked down Bacon Street and up Ninth Avenue until I came to her home. It was raining and she didn't want to go outside for a walk. I sat on her couch and she sat in her chair. It was really Dad's chair but she claimed it after he died and after she spent six months in the hospital recuperating from a stroke. The day I took Mom home from the hospital, Angenita, her occupational therapist, met us there. Angenita was kind but firm. Too much furniture. Too many loose rugs, coffee tables, end tables, small bookshelves, Dad's smoking stand. Except for some of the large furniture, everything had to go. Too many corners on which to hit her head if she fell.

Bill and I carried the furnishings to the basement. Piece by piece it all vanished. Until it came time to take Dad's La-Z-Boy chair downstairs. "No. Not Dad's chair," she sobbed. "You can't take Dad's chair."

So we took the good chair, the one that matched the couch, downstairs.

As I sat on the couch that rainy afternoon, I suggested that I make an appointment with Doctor Coburn for her next week.

"You'll have to take me, then," she said. "Nancy is working next week."

For the first time in eight years we didn't go to Baja. We stayed home. Most evenings we walked, bundled up against the north coast winter, searching for darker, quieter routes so the house lights and car lights and streetlights wouldn't dim the stars and the progression of the moon. Eighth moon, quarter moon, half moon, full moon. The same moon, same constellations, same appeal in Prince Rupert that we surrendered to in Baja, four thousand miles away.

—

"There's a letter on the kitchen table from Matilda," Mom said.

"Matilda?" I asked.

"You know who I mean."

I didn't know, so I walked into the kitchen and looked at her mail. There was a letter from her sister-in-law, Sheila, and a blue airmail letter from her cousin, Valerie, in England. She had never met her English cousin but corresponded with her for years. She referred to her as Cousin Valerie as if it were her title. Like Queen Elizabeth.

"Oh, you mean your Cousin Valerie."

"No, no. Matilda."

"Sheila?" I asked.

"No. You know. The people who had a store in Alberta when Dad had the creamery there. We were all newlyweds. We were friends for years."

"Roebucks? You mean Eleanor Roebuck?"

"Yes! I got a postcard from them from Alaska. I put it on the front of the fridge."

"Mom, Bert Roebuck died years ago and Eleanor lives in Ontario with her son. I don't think she'd be well enough for a trip to Alaska."

I was thinking of the last time Mom received a Christmas card from Eleanor Roebuck. The letter inside, written by Eleanor's daughter-in-law, told of the advancing Parkinson's disease. It had taken Eleanor half a page to sign her name under her daughter-in-law's tidy writing.

I took the card from under the fridge magnet. "It's from Angenita," I said as I walked back into the living room. "Your occupational therapist."

"What's she doing in Alaska?" Mom asked.

"Probably on holidays," I answered. The picture on the postcard showed white sand, turquoise sea and palm trees.

—

I have a theory that baby turtles make a run for the ocean when there is no moon and the tides are big. One winter Bill and I had camped at Bahia de Los Frailes, a postcard perfect bay on the Sea of Cortez side of southern Baja. Late one afternoon, at low tide, we went for a long walk to the farthest point north on the bay. Coming back, we walked high up on the beach, close to sandy banks. We noticed an area where sand was churned up. Small tracks littered the area, going in every direction, but all eventually turning towards the sea. About twenty feet away all tracks disappeared, erased by the last high tide.

"I bet it's baby turtles," I said to Bill.

Late that night we walked back down the beach. There was no moon. When we got close to the sandy banks, we turned on our flashlights. It wasn't baby turtles that hid from the light. "It's sea crabs," Bill said. "They borrow empty shells on the beach and come up looking for food. There must have been tenters here."

—

Mom and I were outside for her daily walk. She struggled up the ramp, hanging onto the railing with her right hand and all her weight on the four-pronged cane gripped by her left hand. She turned at the top and headed down again. She was almost at the bottom when she stopped and looked at me. "I had a visit from the minister today," she said. "Are you interested in having my piano?"

"I never thought of it," I answered. "Why do you ask?"

"The church has two or three pianos but they are all badly out of tune and probably not worth spending money on. I thought if you didn't want the piano I would give it to the church."

"You mean you would sell it to the church."

"No. I don't want to sell it."

"I can't stand the idea of you not having your piano, Mom. Your father bought it for you when you were a child. You've played that piano for as long as I can remember."

"Well, if no one in the family wants it, I might as well give it to the church."

"No one in our family would dream of asking for your piano. You're a music teacher."

"What happens when I can't live here anymore? I'm going to have to make some decisions soon. What am I going to do with all my furniture?"

"Where are you going?" I asked.

"I don't know," she answered.

She finished her laps and held my hand as she made her way into her front porch. Her right foot caught on the doorjamb and she couldn't pull her foot inside. "Oh, come on now! Don't you start acting up on me, too! Come on! Come on! COME ON!" She hollered at her foot as if the strength of her words would pull the foot inside. "That's better," she said as her leg dragged her foot into the porch. She hung onto the pipe railing Bill had made for her and hauled her body up the half step he installed.

"I'm not ready to go to The Manor yet," she said as she settled into her wheelchair. "They are all sick up there."

I walked home and cut the grass. I was about half way down our back yard when an idea hit me. She wouldn't give her piano away if she still had music pupils. She had resumed teaching piano and theory after recovering from her stroke and had taught until she was almost eighty-four. It was a year since she decided to stop teaching. "I don't want to start something I can't finish," she had said.

After I cut the grass, I showered and walked back to Mom's. "Will you teach me how to play the piano?" I asked.

I couldn't believe it was me playing *Twinkle, Twinkle, Little Star.* "Say the notes out loud as you play them," she told me.

"F, f, c, c, d, d, c. B, b, a, a, g, g, f."

While I played and recited the notes, she counted, "1, 2, 1, 2, 1, 2, 1, 2, 1, 2, 1, 2, 1, 2, 1, 2. Give those whole notes their full two counts," she said. "Don't lift your fingers too soon."

Once a week she gave me a lesson and every day after our walk, I went into her music room, closed the door, and practiced. For the first several weeks the TV blared in the living room. Then one day I noticed silence. I continued practicing. "B flat," she shouted from her chair in the living room. The next day I heard her wheelchair squeak outside the music room door. When I finished practicing, I got up, turned off the light and opened the door. She wheeled her chair backwards so I could leave the room. "Don't forget to keep your tempo even," she said. "You can't speed up for the easy parts and then slow down for the hard parts."

I moved the piano stool out of the way for my lesson so she could take a wide swing with her wheelchair to get her legs under the keyboard. Then I placed the stool against her chair. I had worked hard at theses pieces. I really liked them. They were from *The Burnam Book: Ten Solos for the Young Pianist*, by Edna Mae Burnam. The copyright was 1958. I always looked for the copyright when I started a new book. If Dorothy Thornton was written in her fine handwriting on the top of the book, I knew the copyright was earlier than 1932, when she married Dad. The copyright on her hand bound volumes of Beethoven's sonatas was 1894.

Mom had listened to me practice two pieces from *The Burnam Book* for a week and when I came out of the music room had said, "Very nice. Those are starting to sound very nice. Watch your expression. Not so loud on that last piece. Autumn leaves don't come crashing down."

While I played those two pieces during my lesson she never said a word. No interruptions, no corrections. When I finished, she leaned back and said, "Thank you."

We played our weekly game of Scrabble. I had no vowels. I had the Q, an L, F, two V's, a C and the Z.

"I can't go, Mom," I said. "You go."

"You must have something," she said. She turned the wooden tray that held my letters towards her. Her father had made the Scrabble board, the little trays and the letters after he retired from his job as proofreader for the Calgary Herald. Every square on the board was lined out with his wood burning set. The double words, triple words, double letters, triple letters were etched into the wood with his careful, shaky printing. Each individual wooden square letter was engraved with an alphabetical character and its count.

"You have clef," she said. "Use that E that's open near the bottom."

"Clef?" I asked. "C, L, E, F?"

"Yes," she answered. "It's a symbol used in music to indicate the pitch of the notes on the staff."

"Oh. Thanks."

—

I arrived at Mom's to take her for her walk and to practice the piano. She was dressed in her best pink blouse and a skirt. She wouldn't go for a walk. She was sitting in her wheelchair in the middle of her living room watching The Boston Pops Orchestra on TV. I set a chair beside her and sat down. The chair shouldn't have been upstairs. But piece by piece furnishings had gradually appeared. She must have asked Eva, her homecare worker, or guests, to bring the items from the basement. When I first noticed it happening, I carried them back downstairs. But they never stayed there. Her big chair was her only concession.

The performance on TV had film clips of Bing Crosby and Louis Armstrong. The music they made famous was played by the orchestra and special guests. Mom was right in the concert hall. She clapped and laughed with the rest of the audience. Tears stained her pink blouse.

—

We were in Baja when Mom had suffered her stroke. She didn't feel well and, not wanting to bother anyone on the weekend, had gone to bed. Eva found her on Monday morning when she arrived to do the laundry. For the next few weeks Mom was in a hospital bed not able to move or talk.

Bill and I were camped in the best campsite we ever had in Baja. It was the winter of 1989 – 1990, the last winter camping was allowed on the southern beaches between Cabo San Lucas and San Jose del Cabo.

A few days before Christmas we drove into Cabo after supper to phone Mom. A young woman placed our collect call to Canada. I picked up the phone in a small booth and yelled, "Hello, Mom!" A strange voice answered and it took several seconds to comprehend what was being said.

Bill knew something was the matter as soon as I turned around. Tears spilled onto my T-shirt. We had to drive back to our campsite to pick up the address book. I didn't know, or couldn't remember, my brothers', daughter's or son's phone number. We picked up the address book and drove back to Cabo. This time Bill had the collect call placed to my eldest brother, Vince.

The drive back to our campsite was slow. There was no moon and we couldn't see cattle on the road until they appeared in the glow of our headlights. Bill told me what my brother had said. It didn't look good but Vince insisted that there was no need for me to fly home. There was nothing I could do. She was in expert hands. Vince said the family was going to take turns flying to Prince Rupert to be with her, and that my children were going home for Christmas. He said she would need me more in the spring.

We had a wonderful winter that year. We swam, hiked, walked and socialized. It's funny how the mind can block out sadness for hours when you're having a good time. It was in the evening, in front of a fire, watching scorpions scurry from the mesquite thrown into the flames, gazing at the moon as it rose from the ocean and cast its light on the long curl of the surf, when my emotions staggered between sorrow and anger. Mom had looked after Dad for eight years before he died. Eight years without a holiday. One by one her pleasures eroded. She stopped walking to church to practice the organ. Shortly after, she stopped playing the organ for the Sunday service. She didn't want to play if she couldn't practice. She taught fewer and fewer music pupils. She seldom left the house unless I took her shopping or kept Dad company while she went to a church tea or a piano recital. After years of looking after Dad, she finally had a chance to travel, to visit her family, to go for lunch with her friends, or go for a coffee after a concert. But two months after Dad died, a stroke took her chance away.

I wrote her lots of letters that winter and when we were in Cabo, mailed them at the small post office. While I was there, I checked the board where general delivery mail was listed. I savoured news from home. I carried letters in my pockets and often sat and read them when I went for a walk or hike by myself.

On our way north at the end of the winter, we stopped at the post office one last time. Inside the tiny room I searched the lists for my name. I saw a Nancy Roberts. I went to the counter and asked for mail for Nancy Robertson. The clerk searched one drawer, then another. Finally he took out a letter, showed me the front and questioned whether this one was for me. I didn't recognize Mom's handwriting but I saw Borch and her address in the upper left hand corner of the envelope. The last two letters of my name had a postal stamp covering them so it was easy to understand why it had been listed and filed as Roberts. My hand shook as I reached for the letter.

I had a hard time reading the letter out loud to Bill. Mom's writing was difficult to read and I had to stop often to wipe my eyes. It was a newsy letter, telling of my brothers' and children's visits. She said that my son had sent twelve letters to her piano students giving them notice that she did not know when she would be teaching again, and giving the names of three or four teachers. She said it was a very hard letter to send. She wrote about her therapy, and re-educating her muscles. We laughed uncontrollably when I read it took her over a week to get a satisfactory shrug and again when she wrote about the wheelchair and trying to use the elevator by herself. "I usually miss one or two elevators as I don't get the chair off or on fast enough," she said.

—

The letter was a gift to me, and every year she has lived since has been another gift. Sometimes the ribbons and wrappings are difficult to remove. There are days when I wish I didn't have to take her for a walk or to a doctor's appointment. I wish I didn't have to do her shopping or cut her toenails. But the alternative is unspeakable. The harder I work at keeping her well, the longer I will have her with me.

—

The Sunday before Easter, I picked Mom up for supper. The volume on her tape deck was up so loud she didn't hear me arrive. A choir sang a passage from the *Messiah*. She was sitting in Dad's chair, eyes closed, music swirling around her. I wondered if, in her mind, she was the organist exacting such strength from the organ, or the conductor demanding such force from the choir.

I sat on the couch and sang softly with the choir, the words embedded in my memory. I had grown up with this music, Christmas and Easter. When the tape shut off, I helped Mom on with her coat and out to the car.

We ate our supper then cleaned up the kitchen. Routine established a lifetime ago. Sometimes we chatted and sometimes we never said a word, just listened to music.

Just as we had done for years, after the dishes were finished, we played a game of Scrabble. I put my old favourite tape, BEETHOVEN, *Moonlight, Pathetique & Appassionata Sonatas*, in the tape deck. The passion of the piano keys mingled with the clash of the wooden Scrabble letters in Dad's old blue Players tobacco can as we reached in for more letters.

When the tape clicked off, I got up and turned it over. The familiar notes of the *Moonlight Sonata* began. "Remember, Mom," I said, "remember I always asked you to play that for me when I was growing up."

"Yes," she said. "I bought all the popular sheet music in those days, *In the Mood*, *Deep Purple*, but no matter what I played, when I was finished, you always asked for the *Moonlight Sonata*."

"You played it for my children, too."

We listened to the measured strains of the pianist. "I often wonder if I played it that well," she said.

"Definitely," I replied. She never rushed. Every note was given its full count, her expression sometimes powerful, sometimes tender, the tempo always steady, controlled.

"Thank you," she said as she reached for my hand. "If you keep practicing you'll be playing it for your grandchildren, too."

We smiled at one another and sat holding hands until the final note of the sonata faded away.

Bill drove Mom home. I sat in the back seat with leftovers in a casserole dish in my lap. When we got to Ninth Avenue, Mom exclaimed, "Look! The moon's coming up!"

"Yes," I said, "next weekend's the full moon."

The April moon. Close to earth, rising over Ninth Avenue. Just like it did last year. Just like it has every year.

Casualties of an
unprotected heart

I picked Mom up for Sunday supper. We had just started eating when the phone rang. It was my brother, Gerry. "Sheila has lung cancer," he said.

Sheila was our aunt, Mom's sister-in-law. Gerry was worried about telling Mom.

"I will tell her," I said.

We were quieter than normal while we ate. Bill was not teasing Mom and me like he usually did. Mom was not asking questions. There was no mistaking a bad news phone call. I waited until we finished dessert before saying, "It's Sheila. She has lung cancer."

"Oh, no," said Mom.

"I'm sorry I have to tell you."

It was only a few weeks earlier that I had to tell Mom her eldest son was in the hospital in Edmonton after suffering a heart attack. My sister-in-law had phoned the night before. When the phone rang at ten o'clock, and I heard Carol's voice, I knew it was bad news. Vince and Carol always go to bed early during the week, and ten o'clock our time was eleven o'clock their time.

"First thing is that Vince is all right," Carol said. "But he's in the hospital. I think he's had a slight heart attack."

A pain shot through my chest. My right hand pressed against my left breast. I felt my heart beating while Carol talked. I hung up the phone an hour and a quarter later. Twice during the night I woke when pain jabbed my heart. It was hard to go back to sleep. This was my brother. This wasn't a commentary on the radio, or an article in a magazine about heart disease.

It was too late for Carol to phone Mom so I promised to tell her.

—

I was almost fourteen when Vince brought Carol home to meet the family. I was infatuated with her. She was the sister I had longed for.

Years later Carol came for one of her summertime visits. Her daughter, Cynthia, who was thirty-four at the time, came with her. Cynthia's husband had left her and their three children earlier that year. The children were with their father for their first two-week, custodial visit. This was the first time Cynthia had been separated from her children.

My son, Clinton, came home for a visit at the same time. We talked lots about family. How relatives interconnect, like freeways in a city. How we look at things depending on what highway we are on, and who our travelling companions are. We had a wonderful time together. The talking and laughing. The crying and sharing. We walked nature trails and the waterfront. We skipped rocks and looked for shells. We sat on logs at Grassy Bay and beside the waterfall at Diana Creek. Mom joined us for suppers and evenings together, capped off with a game of Chinese checkers.

One evening when we were eating supper, the phone rang. It was Vince. He phoned every evening to talk to Carol. We were together around the table so we all talked to him. His wife, his daughter, his mother, his sister, his nephew, his brother-in-law. Each of us with our own, and different, relationship with this man. When Mom took the phone, she said, "Hello, dearie." Throughout their conversation this endearment slipped off her lips like a sparrow's song in summer.

Cynthia smiled while she listened to her grandmother talking. "I've never heard Dad called dearie before."

My son asked me later that night why I called him Nin. I had called him Nin or Ninny or variations, such as Nin-come-poop, since he was a baby. When he was a teenager, he begged me not to call him anything but his real name. I tried to remember, especially if his friends were around, and although I stopped the teasing names, Nin stuck. When he asked me why, I told him that his sister, who was twenty months old when he was born, couldn't say Clinton. She called him Nin. I think that is the reason. It sounds logical to me but I can't remember. Yet I remember the ride to the country hospital on gravel roads in the early morning darkness at speeds over one hundred miles an hour because his dad, who delivered breech calves and pulled colts, was terrified to deliver a baby.

Mothers tuck tiny details of their children into their hearts, like miniature photographs in small lockets. When Vince left home to go to university, Mom sat for weeks by the dining room window looking out at the fruit trees.

I was eight years old when Vince went to university. That autumn I was always the first one home from school. I ran through the front doorway and yelled, "Hi, Mom, I'm home." The screen door slammed behind me. I ran straight to the kitchen and if she wasn't there, I looked outside to see if she was in the garden.

After a few days I stopped looking for her and ran directly to the dining room. She was just sitting. She wasn't doing anything. No mending or sewing. The radio wasn't on and she wasn't reading. When I came alongside her, she put one arm around me, lifted her apron with her other hand and wiped her eyes. "How many times do I have to tell you not to slam the screen door?"

━

When my daughter, Shirley, left home to go to university, tears stung my eyes unexpectedly, constantly. One of the women I worked with was on maternity leave. She brought her new baby to the office. I left the crowd gathered around her and returned to my desk. I bent over papers but the figures blurred.

Mom phoned one evening and asked, "How are you doing?"

"Awful." I told her about watching children the first day of school. New jeans, running shoes, haircuts. How I had to pull the car over to the curb because I couldn't see to drive.

"I thought you might be feeling that way. That's why I phoned," she said. "I missed you terribly when you left home."

━

I waited to tell Mom about Vince until we were outside for her daily walk up and down the wheelchair ramp. I tried not to be blunt. I wanted to spare her any pain. I started by saying, "Carol phoned last night."

"Oh, how's everything going with them?"

I tried Carol's tactic. "First thing is that Vince is O.K."

She stopped halfway up the ramp and turned and looked at me. "What's the matter?"

"Vince is all right, Mom, but he is in the hospital. He's had a slight heart attack."

"That's too bad," she said. She resumed her walk. She started off with her left foot and her four-pronged cane. "That's too bad." She dragged the weak right leg until it was alongside her left leg. She stepped forward again with her left leg and cane. "That's too bad." The right foot followed. Every time she moved her strong foot, she said, "That's too bad." Drag. "That's too bad." Drag. "That's too bad." Drag.

A car pulled up in front of Mom's house. A woman we didn't recognize got out and asked, "Did you notice an ambulance across the street at 4:30 this morning?"

Mom shook her head.

"No," I said to the woman. "Is everyone all right?"

"My daughter-in-law's heart stopped at 4:30 this morning. She had a sinus infection and somehow her lungs filled and her heart stopped. Good thing my son knows CPR and good thing the ambulance came right away."

"Oh, dear, that's terrible. Is she going to be O.K.?" I asked.

"We don't know. They medevac'd her out and operated on her sinus but she's still unconscious. They won't know if there is any damage to her heart or to … She's only thirty-one. She's never been right since she had the baby. Always sick. We have the baby and the other two children are with friends. Hard to have a baby around at our age."

Mom and I listened to this woman unburden her fears. Strangers make the best listeners and strangers tell the best stories. Like a child's wind-up toy, she wasn't going to stop until she stopped and we weren't going anywhere until she finished. Mom is hard of hearing so she moved down her ramp and closer to the woman. This was a change in Mom's routine. She was included. This news would not come to her second hand.

Finally the woman stopped talking and looked at her watch. "I'd better hurry," she said. "I came for some of the children's things. The baby was sleeping when I left. My husband is looking after him. I'd better get back before the baby wakes."

She crossed the street and disappeared into the house leaving her intimacies behind. Mom and I walked up the ramp and stepped into the front porch. I helped her take her coat off and I hung it on a hook.

"It's sad," I said, "only thirty-one. There's just no telling is there, Mom?"

"No," she said, "there is no telling with matters of the heart."

—

When I was in my early thirties, I bought Mom a bouquet of roses on Valentine's Day. This was totally out of character. I was busy with my life and usually forgot special occasions. When I gave Mom the flowers, she cried.

"I'm sorry." She wiped her eyes. "This has always been a bad time of year for me. This is when Karen died."

Karen was my sister. She was born four years after me. She only lived seven weeks and she never left the hospital. I remember Mom telling me about Karen when I was a girl. How, if she had lived, she would have spent her life in a wheelchair. Mom said that it was probably best that she hadn't lived. At the time, I was mad. I wanted a sister so badly I would have taken one on any terms.

Here was Mom, so many years later, mourning the loss of her child. She told me, "There are some things the heart never forgets."

—

I never touched or held my first child, Michael, born eight weeks early. He was whisked away at birth and placed in an incubator. He only lived twelve hours. I didn't know he had died until the next morning when a nurse came into my room and said, "You'd better hurry and make funeral arrangements before the weekend." When I looked at her, she staggered backwards clutching her chest as if I'd shot her.

"Didn't anyone tell you?" she asked.

"No," I answered.

I lay back on the bed as she scurried from the room saying, "I'm sorry. I'm sorry."

The Beatles were singing from my small transistor radio on the bedside table, "Michelle ma belle, these are words that go together well, my Michelle."

Tears came when the Beatles continued singing, "I love you, I love you, I love you, that's all I want to say."

My relationship with the baby's father ended and I married someone else on the rebound. He knew about the baby, had lent me money to pay the funeral home. He was tall, dark and handsome and had a wonderful personality and sense of humour. Our life together might have worked out if he hadn't been a binge drinker. Every few months he would get drunk for two or three days. He lost jobs and we moved often. He was a fine man sober but a violent man drunk. In the early years, after a binge, I believed his promises that he would never drink again.

I had not told my family about my pregnancy before I was married. Now I did not tell them about the drinking and abuse in my marriage.

After six years of marriage, and after a drunken beating in front of my cousin, Sylvia, I told him I was leaving. He threatened to tell my family about the baby if I left him. A year later I left with two children, eight boxes and my trunk, saying, "I don't care. Tell."

When my two children were young teenagers, I told them I had had a child before I married their dad. I wanted to keep that information on the high shelf in the back cupboard of my heart, but I worried that they might find out on their own and have trouble believing anything I might tell them about love, sex and birth control. I told them the first love often hits the heart like an earthquake, altering the landscape forever.

"Damn! Damn!" exclaimed Clint. "Why didn't he live? I always wanted a brother!

—

When Clint left home to go to university, I didn't think I could bear it. The house was so empty. All the aggravations were gone. Like too many phone calls, always for him, too late at night or at mealtime. Too much of his mess cluttering the house. Clothes draped over chairs, banister, bed, floor. Too many records and tapes left lying around, the stereo always left on.

After the flurry of packing, forgetting, reminding, he was gone. I washed his sheets and towels. I threw away the crumpled paper, the single sock, the empty chip bag in the TV room. I vacuumed the dust under his bed, crumbs under the kitchen table and wet grass dragged across the rug from the many trips out to the car with his bags and belongings. I windexed the glass on the stereo. I felt like I was rubbing away the last visible signs of my son. Once his fingerprints were gone, he was, too.

—

After I took Mom home from Sunday supper, I phoned Sheila. There was a strange beeping sound after the second ring. I hung up. I didn't want to wait to phone her. I didn't want to think about what I was going to say. I tried one more time, but the same strange sound happened again. I would have to phone her in the morning.

I didn't sleep well. Dreams had me hanging off cliffs, unable to find toeholds. There was no way to safe ground.

I slept in and phoned Sheila at ten o'clock. I hoped the phone call wouldn't get through. When the ringing started, I hoped no one would answer.

When I heard, "Hello?" I knew the voice.

"Hello, Sheila. It's Nancy," I said.

"Oh, hello, what are … why are … well how are you?"

"I'm fine. But I've heard that you aren't well."

"Where did you hear that?"

"Gerry phoned last night."

"How did he find out I have lung cancer?"

"Bad news travels fast, Sheila."

"I didn't want anyone to know."

"If you didn't want anyone to know you wouldn't have told anyone."

"I suppose you're right," she said. "But I don't have much longer anyway. I'll be gone by the end of the year."

"I'm sorry to hear that. I phoned to say thank you for being so good to me all those years ago."

"I wish things could have been different," she said.

"Me, too."

—

Sheila married Mom's brother, my Uncle Johnny. Johnny survived all the perils of World War Two only to die six years later of leukemia.

Sheila phoned Johnny's parents and siblings when he got sick. They all went to see him, their fun loving son, their reckless youngest brother. He was mad at Sheila for calling his family. He didn't know he was going to die until they all arrived.

He left behind his wife and two young daughters. Sheila was pregnant when Johnny got sick. She lost her infant son, then her husband and then her younger daughter, Robin, was killed in a car accident.

Anne, her older daughter, was four when her dad died. She was happy when her mother married Ray a few years later. She had a dad again, like her friends. Only her new dad wasn't like her friends' dads. From the time she was eight until she was thirteen, she wished she didn't have a dad at all.

Sheila didn't believe her daughter. Sheila said Anne was reading too many books.

—

Sheila and Ray opened their door to me and my young children. I always had a place to stay when my husband was on a drunk, or, after that, between jobs. They lent me money when I needed food. Uncle Ray was always happy to see us, always bouncing Shirley on his knee when I came into the living room.

After Anne had her first daughter, Sheila and Ray visited her. Anne told her mother that she was welcome to stay but Ray was not. Anne said she didn't want him around while her daughter was growing up. Sheila stormed from the house saying if Ray wasn't welcome she wouldn't be visiting either. She did not see her granddaughter's first tooth, first shaky steps, first day of school. She did not see her second granddaughter as an infant, a toddler, a teenager. She did not contact her daughter when she heard that Anne's third child, a son, died an infant crib death.

As a child, my daughter seemed quiet and shy, but there was a depth in her that bypassed silliness and stupidity. When she was twelve years old, she begged me to let her make a trip back to Alberta. She wanted to go to our old hometown and see her friend who had lived next door to us. Mrs. Green was over ninety and had continued to correspond with Shirley the six years since we moved away. I didn't want her to go. But she was determined.

I phoned Sheila and asked if Shirley could stay with them a week, and while she was there, would they take her to see the people and places that were embedded in her heart. Arrangements were made and she left by train one gray, coastal morning.

Shirley phoned me the fifth day of her trip. She said she was coming home the next day. I told her to check her ticket, have Auntie Sheila check her ticket. I told her the ticket was for the day after tomorrow.

Sheila drove Shirley to Edmonton the next morning, dropped her outside the train station, said she couldn't stand goodbyes, and left. Shirley sat in the train station by herself all that day. At closing time, one of the ticket agents left her counter, walked over to Shirley and asked what she was waiting for. Shirley said, "My train." The woman asked to see her ticket, then took her home and phoned me.

I phoned my cousin, Sylvia, in Edmonton. I asked her to get Shirley, keep her for the night and make sure she got on the train the next day.

I couldn't sleep that night. Why did I let her go? I should never have let her go.

She arrived home safe and sound on the outside.

We were addressing Christmas cards at the kitchen table later that year. I was sending one to Sheila and Ray, and one to Anne and her family. I said it was sad that Anne didn't get along with her mother. I said Anne was lucky to have a nice guy like Ray for a stepfather.

"I don't blame Anne!" she cried. "I hate him! He's awful!"

—

After my children left home, Bill and I started travelling in the winter. Sheila spent the winters in southern California. Ray had died the previous year of lung cancer. I told Bill I would like to see Sheila, that we would be driving within a few miles of her mobile home.

Sheila was cranky. She missed Ray and she was mad at Anne. She was upset that Anne had not tried to reconnect the family. She was annoyed that I had not kept in touch. She said Ray was disappointed in me and my children. She said that we had not been polite when he had last seen us at my parent's golden wedding anniversary. After that, she told me, Ray would never drive to the coast to visit us. She started to cry.

"Ray was a good man, wasn't he?" she asked.

I couldn't answer. I wouldn't lie and betray Shirley and Anne. There was nothing I could say that she didn't know but would never admit to. We left the next morning and I never saw her again.

After her mother got sick with lung cancer, Anne cared for her. She was with her when she died. Sheila never said, "I'm sorry." Or "I love you." Or "I believe you." She left her money to an old couple who lived next door and left Ray's ashes to Anne.

I started hooking a rug after my children left home. The colours I chose for the mountain were dark greens and browns. The water was murky blues. After two years, red, yellow, and orange-leaved trees appeared. Sometime after that, blue sky came into view and finally bright, multicoloured flowers flourished. One evening when Mom came for supper, she saw the rug draped across the end of the couch.

"Who hooked the rug?" she asked.

"I did," I answered.

"When did you start that?"

"After the kids left home."

She looked at me while I put the place mats on the table and brought the plates and cutlery to her so she could set the table.

"You know those braided rugs I had in all the rooms?" she said. "I started making those after you children left home."

I dished the food into serving bowls and carried them to the table. Bill opened a bottle of red wine. We joined Mom at the table.

"I wonder who'll phone tonight," she said.

Bill poured the wine. We raised our glasses for our usual Sunday toast, like a grace, "Here's to the family."

Our three glasses met and clinked above the centre of the kitchen table.

Thursday afternoon

I knew something was wrong as soon as I saw Mom's drapes open and her house in darkness. Every evening at 9:00 Mom closed her drapes in the living room and front porch, and turned on the lamp on top of her television. It was already 9:15. The last day of August was almost over.

I didn't rush through the open gate and run up her wheelchair ramp. Thursday was her garbage collection day and, aside from leaving the gate open, the garbage men had left the lid off the can. I walked alongside the ramp, picked up the lid, set it firmly on top of the can and placed the can back under the ramp. Every Thursday evening she asked me the same two questions, "Did you put the garbage can back under the ramp?"

"Yes."

"Did you put the lid on?"

"Yes. Yes, I did."

I knew something was wrong and I knew not to run up the ramp and barge into the porch. The police had cautioned me only a few weeks earlier. They had arrived before me when Mom had activated the beeper on her emergency telephone, accidentally, again. She wore the beeper on a cord around her neck and at night tucked the beeper inside her pajama pocket over her heart. So it was at night when our telephone rang, severing dreams, releasing adrenaline, that I ran to the kitchen to answer the phone, hoping to interrupt the sequence of numbers before it woke her friend, Ethel, then her friend, Fran, and finally alerted 911.

Sometimes the ringing woke Bill and me four or five times a night. I would hear the beep of the alarm as soon as I picked up the receiver. I squinted against the harsh overhead light in the kitchen as I punched in the numbers on my phone to squelch the alarm on Mom's phone and activate her speakerphone.

"MOM! MOM! ARE YOU ALL RIGHT?" I would holler, trying to be heard over the alarm I knew was blaring in her living room. I don't know if she could hear the alarm or not. She always said, "I didn't hear a thing," when I arrived at her home in the middle of the night. She would have had to sit up, transfer herself into her wheelchair, find light switches in the dark and work her way through narrow doorways into the living room to stop the alarm herself. It was probably easier staying in bed, knowing I would arrive as soon as I dressed and ran the two blocks to her home.

"What are you doing here?" she asked when she saw me.

"Your alarm woke me. Are you all right?"

"Of course I'm all right."

After several episodes, her response was, "I don't understand why the alarm keeps going off. There must be something the matter with that phone."

"I think you're accidentally pushing the button when you turn over, Mom." I took the cord from around her neck and laid it beside her pillow. "Leave it here while you're sleeping and put it back around your neck in the morning."

We went through the same conversation several times a night. Each time I arrived at her home the cord was back around her neck with the pendant tucked inside her pajama pocket.

One night, the constant ringing worked into my dreams. I couldn't get my legs to move. I could not get to the ringing phone. I don't know how long it took to wake, but I woke to silence. I jumped up and ran to the phone but I was too late. A dial tone. I phoned Mom but the line was busy. Then my phone rang.

"Nancy, does your mom live at 1019 Ninth Avenue East?" a friend asked.

"Yes."

"I've got my scanner on and the police were just dispatched to that address."

"I know. I've got to run. Thanks."

I did know. I knew when I woke to silence. I knew when I heard the busy signal on the phone. I knew I couldn't keep up anymore. I knew I couldn't keep checking several times a day. I knew I couldn't keep running back and forth at night. I knew she'd had enough, too. She apologized constantly for disturbing me, for being such a nuisance.

"I don't know what's the matter with me," she said when she fell. "I don't know what's the matter with me," when she burned her arm on the stove. "I don't know what's the matter with me," when she knocked a lamp over, when she dropped a plate on the floor, spilled milk across the table, couldn't find her glasses, couldn't remember what day it was.

Our conversations were simple now.

"I'm sorry," she said.

"It's O.K., Mom," I replied as I swept broken glass, mopped spilled milk, found lost glasses.

━

As quickly as I dressed and as fast as I ran, the police still beat me to Ninth Avenue. The flashing light on their car broke the stillness of the quiet street. I charged past the two officers who were walking up the wheelchair ramp and I jammed Mom's house key into the lock.

"STOP! YOU DON'T KNOW WHAT YOU'RE GOING TO FIND ON THE OTHER SIDE OF THAT DOOR!"

I don't know if I stepped aside or if I was moved aside, but both officers entered the house ahead of me, slowly opening the door into the porch. Slowly pushing open the glass paneled door, covered with its crocheted curtain, into the living room. The alarm on the telephone blared louder as doors opened. One of the officers stepped across the living room rug and pushed the flashing light on the telephone. Instantly the alarm stopped. But there was no silence. Music poured from Mom's bedroom filling every crack in her rundown wartime home. Scraped doorways, bashed furniture, marked walls, all soothed by a piano and orchestra celebrating Beethoven's *Fifth Concerto*.

Mom sat on the edge of her bed. The volume on her clock radio was turned up so loud she did not hear anything but the music. Her eyes were closed. Her body swayed with the intensity of the music. Her left hand held an imaginary baton and conducted the orchestra from *pianissimo* to *forte*.

She was ready for bed. She had folded her crocheted bedspread and set it on the seat of an old dining room chair that was kept in the bedroom because the back had broken off. She had turned down the white sheet and two thin blankets and was sitting on a worn, fitted, blue sheet. Her purple velour housecoat, a Christmas gift from her daughter-in-law, Carol, lay across the end of the bed. She was wearing a pink, floral pajama top from a new pair of pajamas I found in a bin at Zellers. Constantly on the lookout for double extra large sizes for her, I found and bought two pairs, knowing I would have them when she needed them. She complained when I gave her one new pair. "I don't need new pajamas," she said. "The ones I have are perfectly all right."

Brand new sheets and towels, bath mats and dish cloths, gifts from family members, remained in her linen closet. She used perfectly all right threadbare towels and bath mats. This night she wore faded, blue and white patterned, flannelette pajama bottoms. Her mismatched pajamas and sheets matched the disarray in her bedroom.

Five generations of family photographs crowded walls and dresser tops. Weddings, graduations, family portraits. When Dad was alive, he arranged the photographs logically, tidily. But after he was gone, Mom hammered a nail in the wall wherever there was room. A new great-grandchild appeared in the old Danish family grouping. Three brightly dressed grandchildren smiled beside black and white photos of serious, gowned sons clutching their degrees. The tops of both dressers were covered with photographs in cardboard folders, some standing up, some fallen over. The photos encroached on the space needed to hold a lifetime of family mementos and knick-knacks.

Wool spilled from her knitting basket and her crochet basket wobbled on top of stacks of needlecraft books. The clothes she would wear in the morning were draped across the back of a sturdy chair and dirty clothes had been tossed into a laundry hamper beside her vanity. The double bed, in which they had slept side-by-side for close to sixty years, had been replaced with a single bed to make room for her wheelchair. But Dad's terry cloth housecoat still hung on a hook just inside the open closet. After Dad died, I offered to help her with his clothes.

"I can't bring myself to get rid of his things," she said. So his undershirts, shorts and socks lay tidily folded in his dresser drawers, and his suits, shirts and ties still hung in the closet seven years after his death. The clutter in the room came together like music played by different instruments in the orchestra.

The two officers and I had stood in the bedroom doorway for several minutes while Mom conducted the musicians. The pianist's fingers flew up and down the keyboard complemented by the crescendo of the orchestra. We stood quietly until Mom brought the concerto to a close.

There was a moment's silence. The red numbers on her clock radio showed 11:59. I knew she would listen to the CBC news at the top of the hour before switching the button on the radio so it would come on again at 8:00 in the morning. She liked to be up and dressed and have the drapes opened by 9:00 every morning.

One of the officers stepped into that silence. "Are you all right, ma'am?"

"What are you doing here?" she asked when she saw the first officer. "And what are you doing here?" she repeated when she saw his partner.

"Oh, for goodness sake," she said when she saw me. "Now what's the matter? You're here, too."

"Your alarm was set off again, Mom."

"How could that happen? What's the matter with that cockeyed thing anyway?"

"It's O.K., ma'am. So long as you're all right, that's the main thing," said one of the officers.

"No, it's not O.K. This is ridiculous. You shouldn't have to come and check on me."

"It's no trouble, ma'am. We're happy that you're fine. But you shouldn't be wearing your pendant at night. Why don't you put it beside your radio on the bedside table?"

"What good will that do if I have to get up during the night and use the bathroom?"

"Do you use your wheelchair to get to the bathroom?"

"Of course I do."

"Why don't we tie the cord onto the handle of your wheelchair?"

Mom looked at me. She often deferred to me when questioned by others. It had crept up on me, this insecurity of hers. She wanted me with her for doctor's appointments, when health care workers visited, even when family arrived.

"I think that's an excellent idea, Mom. You always have your wheelchair next to you when you're not in it. You would be able to reach your alarm even if you fell transferring yourself."

"Well, O.K., if you think it will be all right." She lifted the cord from around her neck and handed it to the officer.

—

Finally a solid sleep. When my own clock radio woke me at 7:15, I couldn't figure out where I was. Within seconds I realized there was light around the edges of the blind. I sat up. Mom. I wondered if she was all right. I hadn't seen or talked to her for seven hours.

On my way to work at quarter to nine, I drove by her house. The drapes were still closed. I double-parked and ran up the ramp. I unlocked the door and let myself in. When I entered her living room, she was wheeling herself towards me.

"You again," she said. "What are you doing here? Aren't you supposed to be at work?"

"I'm on my way. Just thought I'd make sure you're O.K."

"Of course I'm all right. Listen, you stop worrying about me. I'm fine. Now get going so you're not late for work."

"I'm on my way. Good-bye." I bent over and gave her a kiss. "I'll open the drapes in the porch for you on my way out."

"No you won't. You leave them alone. I'm perfectly capable of doing that myself. I was on my way to do that when you showed up. Now get going and leave me be."

"O.K., Mom. See you later."

"Bye, dearie. Don't you worry about me now."

For a few weeks a peaceful routine steadied our lives. Bill, who was working night shift, slept uninterrupted during the day, and I could hardly wait to go to bed at night to sleep the deep, dreamless sleep of exhaustion. I drove directly to Mom's after work, just like always, to take her for her walk up and down the wheelchair ramp. Then I practiced on the piano for a half an hour before going home and making supper. Bill and I lingered at the table before I packed his lunch and waved goodbye from our back porch window. After the kitchen was cleaned up, I walked downtown for a few groceries. I returned along the waterfront to look at fishing boats and watch seine nets being overhauled. The late sunset over the harbour brought the

day to a close and I walked back up the hill to home and to calm and
to a bed that beckoned with sweet, sweet sleep.

—

Sometimes I convince myself that everything will be fine and
I ignore whatever is niggling at the back of my mind. I knew that
Mom wasn't all right. But I didn't know what to do about it. After
her stroke, Bill and I promised her that we would support her one
hundred percent with whatever she decided. She wanted to go home
so we made it possible with help from doctors, physiotherapists, public
health nurses and home care workers. She was eighty then. Now she
was almost eighty-seven. Things don't change much when you see a
person every day. But when you see someone you haven't seen for a
few years, you think, "Wow, so-and-so sure has put on weight/turned
gray/slowed down/spent too much time in the sun." Little thoughts
and observations so easy for the brain to process from a distance. But
right up close it's not so easy.

Mom still came for supper every Sunday and on special occasions.
I noticed her struggle to get in and out of the car. She couldn't climb
the three steps up to the front porch without Bill helping her. All her
clothes, everyday and Sunday best, displayed permanent food stains.
She licked serving spoons. How could she get sloppy, the woman who
drilled proper eating habits and table manners into her five children.
"Sit up straight and eat properly!"

We still played Scrabble but the words she made, if she could find
them among her letters, were simple and short. The strategy of using
triple words or double letters to increase her score did not concern
her. She was slow counting and our games were long and lopsided. I
didn't want to help her spell and count. I wanted her to do it herself. I
wanted her to stay the same woman who fought back after a crippling
stroke. The woman who never "let" her children win any game. The
woman who hiked all day, came home, ate a big bowl of ice cream,
started supper and ironed until it was ready, while the rest of us had a
nap. The woman who exclaimed, "No! No! No! Not like that!" to her
music pupils until they got the expression right. This might have been
important to me, but she was willing to let herself grow old.

Sometimes there was a smell of urine in her home so I would lecture her about getting up and going to the bathroom more frequently.

"But I don't need to go," she'd argue.

"Obviously you do, Mom. I wouldn't say anything but I know you wouldn't want your friends smelling urine when they visit."

"Of course not! I'll be more careful."

But she wasn't. I tried spending more time with her in the evenings so she could bathe more often. But she didn't feel like it. Or she was watching a special program on TV. "Oh, not tonight, dearie." It was getting harder for me to make her care and I knew she wasn't safe anymore. But I had no solutions except to keep checking on her. I shoved the safety issue to the back of my mind and ignored it. I buried my head in sleep.

—

The last afternoon of August, Bill phoned me at work. He'd been asked to come to work early. "I'll get something to eat downtown," he said, "so you'll have time with your mother."

"No, then I won't see you. I can go to Mom's after supper. I'll come home after work and we can eat together."

After Bill went to work I did the dishes. Then I sat down and read the Daily News. Quiet time alone in the early evening was a rarity and I felt lazy and relaxed and totally without any feelings of obligation or responsibility. I sat for a long time with my head back in the easy chair and my feet up on the footstool. I let the pleasure of silence and stillness flow through me.

When I finally decided to move, it wasn't towards work or duty. It was towards solitude and beauty. I went for a walk into the lovely late summer evening, drawn towards the harbour and the sinking sun that was turning earth to gold and sky to crimson.

It wasn't until dusk settled in that I changed direction and hurried back up the hill. It would be too late to take Mom for her walk but time enough for a visit and a piano lesson.

My peace was shattered when I walked up Ninth Avenue and saw her house in darkness and the drapes still open. Something was wrong but I didn't rush up the wheelchair ramp. I walked alongside the ramp, gathered the garbage can and the lid and set the lid on top of the can. After I had the garbage can stowed away, I walked up the ramp. I slowly opened the door into the porch. The door opened slightly then came against some resistance. I put my head into the opening and saw Mom sprawled out on the porch floor. "Oh, Mom. Oh, Mom," I repeated as I squeezed through the opening and into the porch.

"Nancy? Nancy? Is that you?"

"Oh, Mom. Oh, Mom."

"Help me up, dearie. Come here and help me up."

Her pants were wet with urine and there were two small pools of vomit on the floor by her head. Her white hair was caked with dried vomit. Stepping over her, I ran to the bedroom, grabbed her pillow and pulled a blanket from her unmade bed.

"I don't need that," she complained as I covered her body and slipped the pillow under her head. "Leave the pillow. You're going to get it all messy. I'm all right. Just help me up." She reached for the bar that Bill had installed.

"I can't, Mom. You're too heavy for me and you might have hurt yourself when you fell."

She was still saying she was all right as I phoned 911.

While we waited for the ambulance, I sat on the floor beside her. Details of the accident filled me with guilt. She had not fallen at 9:00 in the evening when she went to close her drapes. She had fallen at 9:00 in the morning after she opened the drapes. She had lain on the floor all day knowing that I would come after work. The one day I didn't come on schedule. The one day I didn't check on her.

"Why didn't you reach up and push your alarm?" The wheelchair was right there in the doorway. I'd had to push it aside to get into the living room.

"I never thought of that."

"Oh, Mom. What about the mailman or the paperboy? What about the garbage men? They were here this afternoon."

"I must have dozed for a few hours. I didn't hear the mailman in the morning. I called out when I heard the garbage men but they were making so much noise they didn't hear me."

"But the paper boy. He threw the paper into the porch. He must have seen you."

"I know, dearie. He asked me what he could do but I told him you would be here soon so not to worry."

"Oh, Mom."

I rode in the back of the ambulance with her. She hadn't wanted to go. She said she'd be fine if the ambulance attendants would just get her into her wheelchair. But with teasing and good humour the medics convinced her that she must be hungry and sore after her twelve-hour shift. They said they knew just the place for her to get something to eat. Mom loved food. They must have realized that when they lifted her onto the stretcher.

She was lucid and cheerful in the ambulance. "It wasn't so bad," she said. "I dozed off and on all day. It really didn't feel all that long." She didn't complain about the long wait in the emergency room. "Why don't you go home? I'll be all right here." She answered all questions and told her story again. She told it again when she was settled into a ward. She was polite and appreciative to everyone. "Thank you. Thank you very much. You've been very good to me."

When all the paper work was completed I looked at Mom lying back in the hospital bed. She seemed so old and frail, despite her two hundred pounds. Without her cluttered belongings surrounding her she looked so alone. White sheets, white walls, pale hospital gown. "Don't worry about her," the nurse said. "We'll take good care of her."

"I know you will," I replied.

When the nurse left, Mom took my hand. "Thank you, Nancy. You're so good to me. But I don't understand why I have to stay here. I'm perfectly capable of looking after myself."

"We'll know tomorrow if you have any broken bones. You're too weak to be on your own. You've been twenty-four hours without anything to eat."

"I am rather hungry."

"I'll run along now. It's getting late and I have to work in the morning. But I'll see you tomorrow afternoon. I won't worry about you tonight. I know you're safe. Goodnight, Mom."

"Goodnight, dearie."

I leaned over and gave her a kiss then put my cheek against hers. We stayed like that for several seconds. The pressure from her hand hurt my fingers as she tightened her clutch on my hand.

When I talked to Doctor Coburn the next day, he told me she was badly bruised on her right side but she had no broken bones. She was already asking him if she could go home. "I'll try and keep her here for a few days, Nancy, but I can't stop her if she wants to go."

I wanted the doctor to tell Mom that she should no longer live in her own home. I didn't want it to be me.

▬

Knowing she was cared for day and night in the hospital brought relief to every waking moment. But at night dreams disturbed my sleep. No matter where I hid, Mom found me. Sometimes I was an adult hiding behind barnacle-covered pilings at low tide and sometimes I was a child crouched in the coal bin. One time Mom would be wearing the royal blue gown she wore when she played the organ at the United Church. Another time she would be in a coat she sewed together out of Dad's old suits. When she found me she started to fall over. I woke when I reached out to stop her.

I knew in my mind that Mom needed more care than I was able, or wanted, to give. But in my heart I knew I could not make the decision to move her into a nursing home.

There was no reason for her to be in the hospital, and she wanted to go home, so she was discharged a week later. I picked her up and drove her home.

She noticed the open gate as soon as we drove down Ninth Avenue. "Those darn garbage men. They left the gate open again. What's the matter with them?"

I eased the car close to the curb and stopped right outside her house. I got her four-pronged cane out of the backseat and helped her out of the car and into her yard. She waited at the bottom of the ramp, clutching her cane and the railing, and watched while I collected the lid and the can and placed the garbage can under the ramp.

"Did you put the lid on tightly?"

"Yes, Mom, I did."

She clung to the railing and struggled up the ramp. She dragged her right foot into the porch. "Oh, it feels so good to be home," she said as I helped her get her raincoat off and hung it on the coat rack. She gripped the pipe railing and pulled her body up the half step and into the entrance of the living room. She turned her body, and hanging onto the railing with one hand, and the arm of the wheelchair with the other, she plopped into her wheelchair.

"Whew," she sighed with eyes closed. "That sure feels good."

I kept my mouth shut. I should have lectured her about the danger of plopping into her wheelchair. She had been taught after her stroke, and reminded regularly, to lower herself into her wheelchair.

"Have you got time to come in for awhile?" she asked as she backed into her living room. "I want to talk to you about something."

I sat on the couch and she wheeled right in front of me until we were knee to knee. Her eyes lowered as she picked at a fresh stain on the front of her pale blue sweater. When she lifted her eyes she took my right hand in both of hers. She stroked the back of my hand while she talked.

"I want you to make arrangements for me to move into The Manor. I want to stay here until the family visits this fall, but when the boys leave, I don't want to be alone. I can't keep it up any more. It's too much for me and it's too much for you. Will you help me."

'Will you help me' was a statement, not a question and I couldn't answer anyway. I don't know if the emotion erupting inside me was relief or sorrow. Years of worry and frustration, and a lifetime of routines and memories that were tied together in her home, ended with the courage of her words. Her strength was my weakness.

"Don't you worry about a thing," she said as she patted the back of my hand. "Everything will work out fine."

Variations

Degrees of Beauty

The *Webster's New World Dictionary* we keep in our trailer describes beauty as "the quality of being very pleasing, as in form or colour."

*W*e are camped at Slab City. This is not a town. This is an area of land about four miles from Niland in southeastern California where hundreds of campers sprawl across the desert every winter. It got its name from the concrete slabs left on the ground when the US military dismantled a desert combat training base used during World War Two. This section of desert is the least picturesque I have ever seen. It is arid and desolate. There are no amenities. Anyone living in Slab City must supply their own shelter, water, power and fuel.

So why are we here? I think the main reason people either camp or live here is because it's free. I think the second reason campers live here for three to four months in the winter is the weather. It is warm and dry. By early March the northern migration of Snowbirds begins as temperatures climb from warm to hot. Even people who don't mind the heat will leave mid-March with sightings of rattlesnakes, scorpions or centipedes, or when mosquitoes, black flies or no-see-ums become unbearable. The deadline for filing income tax pulls the remainder of Snowbirds north in April. Only permanent residents remain in Slab City.

I don't know why anyone would to choose to live here all year. Summertime temperatures are usually over one hundred degrees day and night. So perhaps people can't afford to live anywhere else. Or perhaps a family is waiting for the release of a father or son from the state prison a few miles away. Or perhaps, if you were born here, grew up here, married here and have children here, this is where you want to live. I don't know the reasons people live in Slab City but I do know the number of permanent residents is growing.

Whereas the majority of campers appear to be affluent, arriving in luxurious motorhomes or fifth-wheels and sitting outside in comfortable lawn furniture, all of the permanent residents appear to be poverty-stricken. Some live in tents or cardboard lean-tos, others in hovels made from abandoned lumber or plywood. Some live in their old cars, others in deserted wrecked cars. But most live in dilapidated trailers that have been hauled onto a concrete slab. Most of the permanent shelters are surrounded by junk and garbage. A variety of auto bodies, some up-side-down or smashed, others missing tires and hoods, accumulate alongside beat-up and broken furniture. Garbage is not placed in bags and hauled away but rather flung out onto the slab to pile up with damaged washing machines, stoves and highchairs.

The desolation of the natural landscape and the mess of the man-made landscape is not pleasing, as in form or colour, to my eyes.

What is beautiful? For something to be beautiful does it have to be a grand panoramic scene or natural splendour? Is a rose more beautiful than a dandelion? A peacock's feathers more beautiful than a swallow's? Do we continue to look for beauty if we are born and grow up in beautiful surroundings? Do we have reserves of beauty to last several months? Do we store beauty in our soul like we store calcium in our bones? Does beauty give us strength? Who tells us what is beautiful?

There is an area I call The Corner. It's at the intersection of the main road coming into Slab City, and Low Road, the main road running through the community. There are two big concrete pads at The Corner. Several families of permanent residents have gathered their trailers on and around the two pads. When we first visited Slab City in 1990, there were only two trailers in this area. But a trailer or two has been added every year and now it is a major settlement. To the majority of winter campers, this area is an eyesore.

I pass The Corner every morning on my daybreak walk. After a while my eyes become accustomed to the disorder. I'm curious how the residents of The Corner view the mess, or have their eyes become accustomed to it, too? Do they envy people in fancy motorhomes who drive past them every winter? Or do they find the lifestyle of campers sterile and bleak? Is the placement of their material possessions pleasing, as in form or colour? Who sets the standards for beauty?

As I walk past, a man is sweeping the far end of one of the slabs where a basketball hoop and backboard have been set up on a tall pole. Several teenage boys bounce and pass a basketball back and forth. Once the man has swept the area clear, except for an old jeep body in the centre of their playing area, the boys take shots at the basket. I hear their shouts and laughter as I walk down the road.

My son sends me a small set of watercolours and postcard size paper for my birthday. When I look for something to paint, all nature appears to be sand, beige and other tones of brown. I walk further afield, down into a dried up riverbed or wash, and photograph the clay banks, sandy bottom, trees and shrubs. I want to show my son the challenge he has given me as a newcomer to painting; I will have to make several shades of brown if I am going to paint my surroundings.

But something happens to me in the wash. I look at twisted and misshapen roots and branches of trees. I look at delicate brush with just a hint of green. I am soothed by tones of beige. I'm soothed by silence. When I get back to our trailer I say to Bill, "You know, it's beautiful in the wash."

We are fortunate this winter to have gentle rain five times. In the years we have been visiting friends here I have never seen rain. I have never seen a flower growing. We ride our bicycles along a desert road and I notice a few tufts of grass. I stop and get off my bike. I call Bill. He turns to see where I'm pointing. He looks at the grass then smiles at me.

Several days later, small purple flowers appear, growing out of rippled sand along the sides of desert trails and roads. They spread across the desert floor.

I ride my bicycle back from Niland and notice a spot of yellow. I get off my bike and walk over to a puddle of water. Growing in the middle of the puddle are green leaves. Stretching from the green leaves is a tall yellow flower. At this moment, it is the most beautiful flower I have ever seen. If we have to replenish our soul with beauty, and our surroundings are barren, will a simple touch of beauty be enough to fill our soul?

We have good neighbours in Slab City. One couple, Dave and Dee, have only been married six summers, as Dee says. Dave is seventy-eight. I don't know how old Dee is but I think she is in her early seventies. She looks good, black hair and dark Spanish eyes, and she works at keeping her shapely figure. But there is no denying age, and the skin on her face has lost its youth. We are enjoying Happy Hour together and Dee says, "I want to have a facelift so I would look better, but Dave says I look good."

"That's not what I said," Dave argues, "I said you look beautiful."

Degrees of Fear

The same dictionary describes fear as "anxiety caused by real or possible danger or pain."

I bend over and pick up four sharp-edged rocks, small enough that two will fit in each hand and large enough to startle an approaching dog. I'm afraid of dogs. When I walk at sunrise I carry a cane and put sharp-edged rocks in my pockets.

It's probably a good idea in Slab City to have a healthy fear of dogs. They run loose and sometimes in packs. Two large dogs attack us as we peddle our bicycles along the main road. They back off when Bill throws rocks. We cycle on the road that runs parallel to the Coachella Canal and three large, black dogs appear on the crest of the dune alongside the road. They charge us, growling and barking. Bill tells me to peddle back as fast as I can. He stands behind his bike and challenges them, throwing rocks and yelling. He picks up more rocks and throws them until the dogs stop charging. Bill backs away but continues to throw rocks. Next time we cycle he carries a slingshot.

I am afraid of dogs, but the fear doesn't immobilize me. I still go for a daily walk and I still ride my bicycle. When I'm alone I'm careful where I walk or cycle. I stay on main roadways. I don't go along the canal road or roads where permanent residents live in isolation. They always have several dogs. I don't think I'm paranoid. I'm not the only person who carries a cane. Most people who walk carry a golf club. A few have ski poles or chains.

I also fear poverty. I don't fear becoming impoverished, rather I fear people who, I think, already are impoverished. I don't think this is a healthy fear. I think this is a fear that comes from ignorance. I would like to photograph permanent residents and their living conditions but I can't walk up to someone who appears to be poor, living in isolation, and ask if I can take a few photographs. I think people who isolate themselves from others want to be alone, for whatever reason, and I feel anxiety, caused by real or possible danger, about intruding on their privacy.

My brother, Mike, who knew my childhood fears of being left behind and being left out, would prod me on and make me do things that frightened me by saying, "The worst thing that could happen is that someone might shoot you." I have confronted most of my fears over the years with that memory and it has enabled me to do almost anything. But when I apply that thought to these conditions of poverty, to go where I may not be welcome, I think someone might just shoot me.

Which fear is worse? Programmed fear, imagined fear, excessive fear, sudden fear? Does a lifetime of little insecurities cause as much stress as one main phobia?

Bill and I ride our bicycles along Tank Road, past the campers, and out into the desert. A new pickup truck is parked off the road about twenty feet. A man, who appears to be in his mid-twenties, stands beside the truck. Bill leaves the road, cycles through the sand, stops a few feet from the man and asks, "Do you need a hand?"

"What is opposite?" the man asks.

"Positive, negative," Bill answers.

The man reaches into the back of his truck and swings a pole with a hook on the end. "We are just food for the gods!" he shouts.

I think he is going to strike Bill. But the man starts to walk in circles. He draws in the sand with the hook and talks to himself.

Bill backs away saying, "Take it easy."

———

We are returning to Slab City after exploring desert trails on Bill's big-wheeled motorcycle. We are travelling on a dirt road when a barking dog from a secluded homestead charges us. We are on a collision course whether we speed up or slow down. I think we are going to have a terrific tumble. But we run over the dog, both tires, and keep on going. Bill slows the bike and turns around. "You're going back?" I ask. I see shacks and junk and hear dogs barking.

"I've got to check on the dog," Bill answers.

A man and his wife are tying up the dog when we get there. "I'm sorry if I hurt your dog," Bill says. "I couldn't avoid him."

"I saw what happened," the man replies.

"I've only got four pounds pressure in each tire," Bill continues.

"The dog's O.K.," the woman says. "Thanks for coming back. Most people wouldn't."

Degrees of Poverty

Poverty is "the condition or quality of being poor, need."
Poor is "having little or no means of support, need."

Bill and I live in a seventeen-foot trailer for several months each winter. Three of the seventeen feet is the tongue and hookup area, so living space is fourteen feet. The first time Bill's brother, Robert, looked inside the trailer, he asked Bill, "Where do you sleep?"

Bill pointed towards the bed at the back of the trailer.

"Where does Nancy sleep?" Robert asked.

"Same place," Bill answered.

"How can you both possibly sleep in that little bed?"

In comparison to other campers we look poor.

Is poverty based on comparisons? Is poverty based on appearance? Should the needy look forward to better living conditions in the future? Are you needy if you have less than what you were brought up to expect? When is enough, enough? Who judges who has enough?

I hear on the radio that homeless people should be given a shopping cart to give them a feeling of ownership. I think it is a joke until I read a discarded newspaper in a laundromat. "HOMELESS MAY GET FREE CARTS." Under this headline is written: "A city official has proposed giving homeless San Franciscans free, personalized shopping carts to protect their belongings and cut down on pilferage." This small article reports that a committee met to discuss the plague of abandoned carts on city streets.

I see lineups in the Niland post office the day welfare cheques arrive. I see food stamps being used to purchase groceries at the two small grocery stores, China One and China Two. I don't know the real names of these two stores. Ever since we started to camp in Slab City these are the terms used to distinguish the stores. "Did you buy that at China One or China Two?"

I ride my bicycle to town three or four times a week. I do it for exercise but check our post office box for letters from home and buy two bananas or a half-pound of hamburger while I'm there. It is a safe destination for me. I don't have to worry about dogs on the highway.

Many of the permanent residents also ride bicycles to town. They ride them because cycling is their only means of transportation. Some of their bikes have a basket attached to the handlebar and carriers mounted on the sides and back. The ride to town is easy. It is slightly downhill all the way. But the return trip is a good workout, especially if the wind is in your face. Many of the residents push their bikes home when their carriers are full. Some carry a gallon or two of water on their handlebar as well. I see one man cycling to town holding his handlebar with one hand and a propane tank on his shoulder with the other.

My bicycle is an old, big framed, one speed CCM bike with twenty-eight inch wheels. I peddle backwards to brake. Bill installed an old-fashioned, high-shaped handlebar so I can sit up straight and not aggravate the arthritis in my neck. My bicycle looks poor in the hierarchy of bicycles.

I stand in the lineup at China Two with an onion and two tomatoes. A man walks towards me and says hello. He has long hair, a big beard and wears raggedy clothes. We often wave at one another as we bike to and from Niland.

"Are you camped at The Slabs?" he asks.

"Yes," I reply.

"Where are you from?"

"British Columbia, Canada."

"Man," he says, "I'm impressed. That's a long ride. How long did it take you?"

Degrees of Health

"Physical and mental well-being, freedom from disease. Condition of body or mind."

I hear on the radio that 378,000 dead birds washed ashore on the banks of the Salton Sea. They literally fell out of the sky. When I tell Bill, he says we should get out of here, that birds dying is one of the first signs that something is wrong with the air we breathe.

"No sense leaving," I say. "Look at all the birds that have moved to Slab City."

Every day more birds sing from the creosote trees and dozens more sea gulls squat on the gravel off the main road on my morning walk. A young child from The Corner chases them. He waves his arms and hollers. The gulls flutter a short distance and settle back down just out of reach. I disturb butterflies, so plentiful that when I ride my bicycle they float up and silken wings brush my bare legs.

The Salton Sea is approximately five miles from Slab City. The Salton Sea and Niland are in the northern part of the Imperial Valley. This arid valley has some of the most fertile soil in the US. An extensive canal system has made it possible for crops to be grown year round.

The New River crosses into the US from an area of Mexico where metallic and acid compounds leak into the water from industrial cities. The river flows through the Imperial Valley where innumerable pesticides and insecticides are sprayed over crops, and several huge feedlots taint the landscape. The New River empties into the Salton Sea.

One of the attractions of camping in this part of southeastern California for part of the winter is the availability, variety and quality of fruits and vegetables. It is fun to shop for groceries. Produce looks good and is inexpensive. Carrots, cauliflower, oranges – they taste so much better when we eat them freshly harvested.

We see trucks so loaded with carrots or oranges the produce falls off. Some people glean fields after the harvest, others go directly to packing plants where produce is given away.

I wash everything before we eat it, same as I do at home. But what if insecticides and pesticides have seeped into the food we eat? How many servings of contaminated fruits and vegetables should we eat every day? How many steroids and antibiotics are fed to the livestock and poultry we consume? How long before polluted rivers and oceans poison the fish we eat?

I think I am healthy. I eat well, gets lots of exercise and plenty of rest.

I keep busy. Aside from my bicycle and good walking shoes, I bring all my hobbies with me. I write, photograph, paint, read books and hook rugs. Some winters I'm more industrious than others. A lot depends on the weather. When the temperature stays in the mid-seventies during the day I have a ton of energy. When the temperature climbs into the eighties, I read all afternoon. When the temperature reaches ninety, it is almost impossible for me to cook a meal. By ninety-five to one hundred degrees I lose my appetite and my interest in living. There is no project on which I want to work.

Winter months are pleasant. Even if days become unseasonably hot for a spell, nights are cool. But summer months must be dreadful. At times the temperature climbs to one hundred and twenty-five degrees. Some days are over one hundred and thirty. It cools off to one hundred degrees during the night. I cannot imagine living in these conditions. Does intense heat affect our physical and mental well-being?

I notice that many Snowbirds get impatient after a couple of months in warm climates. In Slab City they drive too fast, raising dust that settles on every surface inside trailers. They ignore freshly washed clothes fluttering on outside lines. They become agitated if they get behind slower moving vehicles or bicycles on the highway to Niland, and roar past at the first opportunity. I feel impatient myself when the thermometer rises into the nineties. My temper flashes when I can't get the generator started or discover a flat tire on my bicycle.

How hot does it get inside a trailer on a concrete slab in summertime? Do you send your children out to play in one hundred and thirty degrees because it's cooler outside? How do you find energy to make nourishing meals? Read bedtime stories? Look for work? How do you keep your body and mind healthy?

An old-looking man has driven to our campsite twice this winter to give us fresh romaine lettuce. He arrives in a truck that coughs and chokes. Although he keeps the engine running when he gets out, it sputters to a stop. I offer him apples in exchange for the lettuce but he won't take them. "I don't want anything," he says. "I can't stand to see food wasted. I drive all over Slab City to give food away when I've got too much rather than throw it away. I'll never forget when I was a kid. Sometimes we went days without anything to eat."

I cycle back from Niland and notice two teenage girls have set up a stand at The Corner and are selling fresh cauliflower and broccoli. I buy a cauliflower and several stalks of broccoli. When I get back to our campsite I have to rearrange our small fridge so I can fit everything inside.

A boy from The Corner cycles up to our campsite. He looks about twelve and wears camouflage pants and shirt. "Are you a marine?" Bill asks.

"No," he answers.

"Do you want to be a marine when you grow up?"

"Yes, I do," he says. "Do you want to buy some cowflowers?"

"I don't know," answers Bill. "I don't think I've ever seen cowflowers. What do they look like?"

The boy opens the bag he has tied to his bicycle so Bill can look inside. "Oh, cauliflower!" exclaims Bill.

"That's what I said," the boy replies. "Cowflower."

Degrees of Hope

"A feeling that what is wanted will happen."

I hope my adult children are happy. I also hope I can maintain my health and avoid accidents so I do not have to live with chronic pain.

Almost all Snowbirds are retired or semi-retired. Many of them miss their homes, telephones, golf courses and grandchildren. Many complain about being bored and having nothing to do. People line up every Sunday at pay phones in Niland. They spend hours talking to children and grandchildren. Why do they travel south every winter? I think they hope to get relief from pain.

For some, the hotter it gets, the better they feel. The last three days have been unseasonably warm. The thermometer has climbed to one hundred degrees inside our trailer. An El Centro radio station reports record temperatures in the Imperial Valley for this time of March. I try to get up by six o'clock to walk in the coolness of the early morning air. I sleep in and don't leave until after seven. It is already too hot for me but I go anyway, knowing it will be the only exercise I will get all day. An old man walks away from his ramshackle trailer. As I pass him he says, "You walk a lot faster than me."

"I've had lots of practice," I reply. "I've been doing it every morning for a few months."

"You're lucky," he says. "I have to wait until the weather is hot. I hope it lasts. It feels so good to get around without my legs hurting."

Do we have any control over hope? Do parents of families living in Slab City hope for better living conditions? Do they hope to someday have a house in Niland with air conditioning? Do they hope their children will stay in school? Get a good education? Or do they just hope it isn't their child who is getting beaten up while waiting for the school bus?

I am almost home after riding my bicycle to town and see an old black truck, which looks like it came out of a Depression movie, stopped in the middle of Low Road. A woman sits in the driver's seat with the truck door open. I stop and ask, "Are you all right?"

"I think I'm out of gas," she replies. "I sent my boy to see if someone around here will give us some. I put two gallons in a couple of days ago. I thought I had enough to drive to town and buy us a couple of hot dogs."

"We drive a diesel truck," I tell her, "but we have a motorcycle. I'll see if we have any gas."

I peddle home and ask Bill if we have any spare gas. He has a one-gallon container that is full so I walk it back to the stalled truck. A big boy, about fifteen, sits in the passenger seat with the door open. The woman is still sitting in the driver's seat. They both get out when they see me coming. By my standards, they look a mess. Shabby clothes, bare feet, unkempt hair, dirty hands and faces, broken nails.

"You didn't manage to find any gas, eh?" I ask.

"No one around here is going to give gas to people like us," the woman answers.

"I have a gallon," I say. "It'll be enough to get you to town to buy more."

The woman reaches for the container but the boy touches her arm. "Here, let me do it for you, Mama." He pours most of the gas into the fuel tank and pours the rest into their container. "Might need some on the carburetor," he says.

The woman hands me two dollars. "We're mighty appreciative, ma'am."

"Keep the money for the hot dogs," I say. "I've run out of gas a time or two myself."

"Thank you. I just hope this truck will start."

Degrees of Happiness

The *Webster's New World Dictionary* does not give a description of happiness. "Happy: 1. lucky, fortunate. Having, showing, or causing great pleasure and joy."

I ride my bicycle under huge power lines that cross over the road high above me on my way to and from Niland. On windy days, wind strums the twelve lines that stretch from gigantic steel poles marching across the desert. They make the ordinary poles, which also cross the highway, look like toothpicks. The twanging lines remind me of home and my friend, Jean. Her husband, Tom, is a musician and I think if he could hear the sound he would write a song about a giant twelve-string guitar playing in the wind and the wild sky of an approaching storm. I can see Jean standing in her front doorway, Tom sitting on the steps, and their two teenagers sitting on the porch railings singing or humming, and strumming real or imaginary guitars.

Thinking about family and friends brings me great pleasure and joy. When I arrive back at our campsite after biking to town, Bill says he can tell by the smile on my face if I have mail in the pouch he has fastened to my handlebar.

Laundry waving in the breeze on sunny days, carrot-stained fingers, suntanned feet, motorcycle rides, coyotes howling in the wash, sitting under a million stars with wintertime friends. Does happiness result from an accumulation of little joys? Is a major happy occasion, like a wedding or birth, equal to many tiny happy occurrences? Does worry about lack of money and food affect our chances of being happy? Is happiness embedded in our memory or our soul?

After a rain, I watch children at The Corner play in puddles. Some run back and forth in bare feet, others stir water with sticks. Two young children squat and splash mud, their diapers sagging into a puddle.

The first sight you see as you come to Slab City is Salvation Mountain. A man named Leonard has been painting a hillside for twelve years. GOD IS LOVE is painted in huge red and pink letters in the centre of the hill, and the surrounding area has biblical verses, birds, trees and flowers painted bright colours. He used to cycle to town most days for food and water but this year he says he doesn't ride as much. "I'm getting too old," he says. "I like the exercise but it's getting harder every year." I see him driving to town, his head bent over the steering wheel, his nose against the windshield.

People arrive in tour buses, cars and motorhomes to see Salvation Mountain. Leonard receives donations of paint and money so he can continue his monument. He tells me he's world famous now and shows me books and magazines with photographs and articles about his project. "I don't know anything about computers," he says, "but I'm even on the World Wide Web. I couldn't be happier."

I cycle back from town after my Sunday morning phone call to Mom and enjoy blue sky and warm wind in my face. I watch two boys on bicycles weave in and out of the yellow dotted line on the highway. One boy looks about fourteen and the other is only about five. As I catch up to them, I say, "Hi!" and wave. The older boy yells, "Race you!" and away we go. I feel like a kid again, flying down the middle of the highway, laughing, with a boy racing beside me. I have the advantage of a bigger bike and bigger wheels, but he has the advantage of youth. I don't know who will finally get ahead because the younger boy who has been left behind cries, "Wait for me! Wait for me!" and the older boy slows down. He hollers at me as he turns around, "I'm going to get me one of those four-wheeled drives!"

Degrees of Regret

"Vt. to feel sorry about (an event, one's acts). Sorrow, esp. over one's acts or omissions."

When my brother, Vince, was sixty-three years of age, he told me that he had never been so happy in all his life. He said the only thing that caused him to lose sleep was the regret he felt for spanking his children.

Regret sounds to me like something from the past. Something that's had a long time to come to the boil. How old do you have to be to feel regret? Is regret healing? Does the acknowledgement of regret bring peace? Are people who live alone or in isolation ignoring something from the past? Still hurting? Hiding their pain?

Although regret sounds to me like something from the past, I regret recent occurrences. I regret not going for a bike ride sooner because company arrives and I feel it would be rude to leave. I regret not having my camera with me when I see two boys, foreheads together, looking at something inside their cupped hands. But recent regrets fade quickly. Regrets from the past simmer for a long time.

When I became a grandmother I noticed my daughter, Shirley, and my son-in-law, Mario, were conscientious parents. I remembered incidents when my children were babies that I had never thought of before. I brought out the old photo album and looked at the few photos of my children in their early years. We couldn't afford many pictures. A roll of film would still be in the camera from one Christmas to the next. I regret not having more photos of my children when they were infants and toddlers.

Inside the album was a picture of me standing in a milking parlour with a cow in the stall beside me and a collie dog at my knees. My ex-husband and I milked ninety cows twice a day for six months. At the time we took this job on the dairy farm, my daughter was two months old. The milking took about four hours in the early morning and about three and a half hours in the late afternoon.

Although I ran back and forth to check on my baby, I regret leaving her for many unattended hours. Did she cry herself back to sleep often?

There is another photo of me in gumboots standing with the cows in the pasture with my daughter in my arms. I know she was happy when we took coffee to the men in the field. I know she was happy in the jolly jumper while I baked and made meals. I know she played happily in the playpen with her fingers and toes. I just don't know how happy she was those hours she spent alone. Did she scream in anger or did her little body shudder with deep sobs?

Does every parent wish they had done some things differently? Does every child wish they could take back some action of their youth? Do we spend too much time beating ourselves up? Should we just acknowledge our sorrow and accept that we did what we did because of circumstances and lack of knowledge at the time?

We are having Happy Hour with our neighbours, Dave and Dee, and talking about our parents. Dave tells us his mother lived with him the last twenty-eight years of her life. He never minded, he says, but his mother always apologized for being such a burden. "I told her she wasn't a burden, and she really wasn't. She had rheumatoid arthritis and was in a lot of pain. I was glad I could help her. I only wish I had spent more time talking with her. I never asked questions. I know nothing about her life or how she felt about it. Now it's too late."

Degrees of Peace

"4. harmony; concord. Serenity, calm, or quiet."

I don't know if I will ever be totally at peace with the reason we travel to warm climates in the winter. Is total peace attainable? Is there a set length of time to recover from trauma? Does misfortune affect our soul? Will enough beauty and happiness bring peace? Or do we have to settle our regrets first? Does lack of peace affect our health? Is lack of peace a reason for our poverty? Our fear? Can we hope for partial peace? Will that be enough for a peaceful soul?

We eat our main meal early afternoon, outside under the awning, usually with a glass of California wine. It's a pleasant time, quiet, no dogs barking or generators running. Only the drone of flies breaks the silence in the heat of the day. After our meal, Bill often stretches out while I clean up the dishes. I put a tape into our small battery operated cassette player and usually listen to pianists playing music by Chopin or Beethoven. I think how lucky I am to be living such a simple, peaceful life.

Many people ask us why we are here. We look young for this way of life. We tell them our jobs are seasonal so there is no point in sitting at home in the rain. We don't tell them we gave up full-time work after a drunk driver ran a red light and totaled Bill's car, smashed his body and changed his life forever. Occasionally someone asks me, "What's the matter with Bill? Why does he walk so funny?" I just say he was in a car accident. I don't like to talk about it. Thinking about the operations, the therapy, the loneliness, the change in our way of life, upsets me. After the accident he said he wished he'd died. He said no one should have to live through such pain. It took him five years to get back on his feet.

In comparison to others, he is lucky. I don't think he feels lucky to have to live in pain. Maybe it's me who's lucky. I'm lucky he didn't die. I'm lucky he rearranged our lives so instead of canoeing and skiing together, we travel. For years we have searched southern California and Baja looking for the warmest place to spend the winter. In return we've had experiences and found adventure.

This winter, whenever we talked about travelling on, another storm hit the coast of California and Baja. The weather was bad in Arizona and snow covered the mountains north of us. So we have spent the winter in Slab City. If anyone had told me, when we first saw this place, that we would spend a winter here, I would have laughed at them. But now it's the second week of April and we're still here. So far, April has been unseasonably cold. Still in the mid-seventies during the day and mid-forties at night. Perfect for me.

Slab City is almost empty. The land looks barren with only a few campers and the permanent residents scattered about. Wildflowers and butterflies have disappeared. Grasshoppers jump out of my way when I cycle across the desert. I know it doesn't matter where I am. I take me with me wherever I go.

Someone is cleaning up at The Corner. I walk past in the early morning and see a huge pile of garbage and furniture. The old jeep body has been hauled off the basketball slab and school-aged children of all sizes scramble for the basketball in a disorganized game while they wait for the school bus. Preschoolers play in the body of an old car. A woman leans against her trailer doorway, her arms crossed one inside the other, watching the basketball game. I smile and wave at her. She smiles back. "Hi, how are you doing today?" she asks.

"Fine," I say. "Just fine, thank you."

The management
of mice

*D*id Grandma's mother help Grandma after the birth of her babies?" my daughter, Shirley, asked me a few days after her second child was born.

"I don't know if Granny helped or not," I answered. "I'll ask Mom when I get home."

I had travelled from Prince Rupert to Penticton by Greyhound bus to be with Shirley after the birth of her sons. Both times I stayed ten days. Both times I spent hours staring out of the bus window when I left. Leaving wouldn't be so sad if I knew when I would see them again. Twenty-seven hours on a bus is a long time.

Perhaps Mom felt the same distance, and sadness of leaving, when she travelled twice by Greyhound bus from Prince Rupert to Edmonton to help me after the birth of my children. She can't remember coming to help me. We had talked about it when I visited her in The Manor before Shirley's second child was born.

"I was so relieved to see you come through the door, Mom," I said. "Shirley wouldn't nurse and she cried all the time. You sure straightened her out."

"I don't remember that, but maybe it was you I straightened out."

"Probably. I didn't know anything about babies. You got me on a schedule and I was fine after you left."

"Did I help you after Clint was born?" she asked.

"Yes. We were working on a ranch outside of Edmonton. We were overrun with mice. For days you set traps and cleaned mouse droppings out of cupboards and drawers. And you chased after Shirley, trying to get her to sit on the potty. You were determined to have her trained before you left so I wouldn't have two babies in diapers."

"Oh, dear. I remember the mice but I forgot the other. I was so worried about you working so hard. Milking cows and all those farm chores. You weren't brought up for that sort of hard work."

I was twenty-three and twenty-five when my children were born. Mom was fifty-eight and sixty when she travelled over twenty-four hours by bus to be with me. After she arrived she rolled up her sleeves and scrubbed and cleaned and taught me routines that last from one generation to the next. Bathing the baby, washing clothes, nap times, walks in the fresh air.

"Feed them before they're hungry and put them to bed before they're tired" was her advice and the same advice I gave Shirley twenty-nine years later.

"Mom, did Granny help you after my brothers and I were born?" I asked when I arrived back home after helping Shirley with her second baby.

"Golly, I can't remember. I'm sure she must have. We were living north of Calgary when I was pregnant with Vincent, and with Gerald, too. I went to Calgary a month before they were born and lived with Mother and Father. I stayed in the hospital at least ten days, maybe two weeks, after they were born. I think it's terrible the way they send mothers home nowadays after just a day or two. That's far too early. How long were you in the hospital?" she asked.

"Five days."

"That's still too soon. Your body needs a rest after that ordeal."

"So you don't know if Granny helped you?"

"I'm sure she must have. But she didn't stay overnight. We would have been living on Seventeenth Avenue in Calgary when Michael and David and you were born. I know a nurse visited regularly after I came home from the hospital and maybe we had the schoolgirls by then."

I remember being told about schoolgirls who helped Mom in exchange for room and board. But Granny's influence remained a mystery. I phoned my brother, Vince, and asked if Granny helped Mom after the birth of her babies.

"Not with any of the grunt work, that's for sure," he answered. "But she was a tremendous moral support for Mom. They talked on the phone every day."

I thought the secret might be revealed in Mom's journals and papers that I had saved and stored in my trunk after dismantling her home when she moved to The Manor. A lifetime of belongings had to be packed or thrown away in less than three weeks, the length of time it took to sell her house. She had never thrown away a church bulletin or greeting card, yogurt container or old pillowcase. Dad had died seven years earlier but his clothes still hung in the bedroom closet.

His cuff links and tie clips still lay in his jewelry case on top of his dresser.

I started in her bedroom, thinking emptying cupboards and drawers and throwing away old clothes would be the easiest. But her bedroom was the most personal. It was in dresser drawers, underneath slips and stockings, where she shoved the love she had trouble demonstrating as we grew up, when she was the firm disciplinarian and task master. Tucked away were clips of infant hair in envelopes with our names written in her tidy handwriting, our baby wristbands from the hospital, our inoculation records, school projects, report cards, ration books issued during World War Two. The drawers also revealed history of her own life – her christening gown and wedding dress, childish cards made for her parents, sweet and loving letters and postcards from her mother, strict letters from her father, a vow to total lifelong abstinence from liquor or spirits, Sunday School projects, correspondence from siblings and friends, censored wartime letters from her brother Johnny when he was overseas, thanking her for writing so often and telling her how he loved to receive her wonderful, newsy letters and parcels. I found journals, scrapbooks, photographs, clippings from newspapers and clothing of mine from infancy to teenage years. I recognized blouses, skirts, dresses, and my hands shook as my fingers stroked and straightened each item. She had kept a blue suit jacket that my son wore when he was four and five because he wanted to be like his Grandad. I had to stop that day.

Every room was the same emotional wrench. Even the basement held details of her life and brought my childhood into my dreams for months afterwards. Inside one of the two trunks in the basement I found the pink, silky bedspread with the matching pillowslip she had made for me. But when my hand touched her old, soft, fluffy housecoat, I knew, before I saw the faded pink and blue material, that I was back in our home in Nelson where I grew up. My hands brought the treasured robe to my face and I buried my head in the folds of the forgotten, familiar scent of my childhood mother.

Vince told me a story a few years ago when we were sitting around the kitchen table after supper. He said that after Mom had Karen, our sister who died a few weeks after she was born, Mom was very ill and stayed a long time in the hospital. I was four years old and Vince was thirteen. He said that when Mom got home, I ran to her crying, "Mommy! Mommy!" and wrapped my arms around her legs. "You and Mom had a special relationship after that," he said.

I don't remember this incident but I do remember getting hit in the face with a softball when I was four. Mom came running when she heard my screams. She gathered me in her arms and carried me into the house but not before the boys got a blast for playing so rough with their sister.

—

I was four when we moved from Calgary to Nelson in the spring of 1948, all seven of us jammed into Dad's 1939 Chevy Coupe. I remember vomiting in the back seat and my brothers being upset that I hadn't said that I was feeling sick so Dad could have stopped the car before I made the mess. I remember, after I started Grade One, running home every recess because I hated school. Mom held me while I sobbed, then took me by the hand and walked me back the two short blocks to Hume School. I remember pitting cherries with her on the back porch steps, helping her sort clothes for Monday wash and, when I got older, being allowed to put clothes through the wringer. All through the elementary grades I ran home after school, got my hug and kiss, then sat on her black stool in the kitchen and talked about my day while I watched her iron, bake, scrub, knit, crotchet. Her hands were never idle.

Through all my young memories, I don't recall Granny ever helping. Granny and Grandad moved to Nelson, too. They came for supper every Sunday except for the occasional Sunday when all seven of us were invited to their small home for a meal that Grandad prepared. Granny baked a cake, a white cake with white icing, every time.

Grandad helped Mom with the huge garden in our back yard and he terraced and trellised his own steep back yard into a work of art. Steps and pathways wound through cascading flowerbeds. He woodworked Chinese Checker and Scrabble boards for himself and his five children's families. He crafted leather purses and briefcases and burned delicate patterns into the leather. He helped Mom with household repair jobs. He scrubbed the bottoms of her pots and her kettle until they shone. While Grandad and Mom cleaned and polished, built shelves and pruned trees, Granny played Patience, a game of solitaire she always won.

While I peeled potatoes and set the dining room table for the Sunday meal, Granny sat and chatted while Mom basted the chicken, prepared vegetables and made the gravy. Granny made us laugh with her stories of what was happening around town. She was full of compliments about Mom's latest preserves and about the new dress I was wearing that Mom had made for me. Granny hugged me lots and told me how pretty I looked. She brought cheer into the kitchen without lifting a finger.

I don't think Granny helped Mom with her five babies and I don't know who helped Granny with her five babies.

Mom never spoke about her grandparents, my great grandparents. It was like they didn't exist, and never had existed. When I searched old black and white photo albums for pictures of them, Mom said, "You won't find them in there." When I asked questions, she asked, "Why do you want to know that?"

But Shirley's question about Mom's mother started me questioning Mom again. Not only about Granny but also about my great grandmother. Who helped Granny?

Mom wouldn't answer. She didn't like my questions. I emailed my cousin, Sylvia, who was working on the family tree, for information about our great grandparents. Sylvia asked her mother, who is Mom's sister, Joyce. Finally I received the information I had been asking Mom about for years. Joyce said Grandad's mother, my great grandmother, died when Grandad was quite young. He had a brother who was taken in by some aunts. His father, my great grandfather, was a drunk and a bum who hung out in the pubs and on the streets of London. Joyce said Grandad, who had no choice but to stay with his dad, also hung out in pubs and on the streets. By the time he was ten or eleven he was an alcoholic from draining all the mugs and bottles. Joyce didn't know if the government stepped in, or what, but he ended up at a church in the Hornsey district of London and lived with a local family. As soon as he was old enough he came to Canada.

Granny's mother, my other great grandmother, also died at a young age. Granny took on the job of cooking and cleaning for the family while her twin sister, Nellie, played. They had a younger sister, Carrie, and a brother, Henry, who, as the story continued, got blown to bits in World War One. Granny's father, my other great grandfather, remarried. Granny had a great deal of difficulty having another woman move in and take over, so she came to Canada.

In London, Granny also attended the Hornsey Church. That is where she met Grandad. They both came to Canada in 1903. Granny was nineteen years of age and Grandad was seventeen. They reconnected in Montreal and were married on December 30, 1908.

Mom was born November 23, 1909 when Granny was twenty-five. They moved to Alberta about a year later. Grandad had one foot turned out and always walked with a limp. Joyce had no idea how or when it happened, but it prevented him from entering the army for World War One. Four more children were born, in 1911, 1913, 1916 and 1918. Who helped Granny with her babies?

I don't think Granny had help with her babies but I think Mom helped her mother as soon as she was old enough. On one of my searches through the old photo albums, when I was trying to find Mom's grandparents, I saw many photos of Granny with an older couple. I said to Mom, "They must be Granny's parents."

"No, they aren't."

"Who are they?" I asked.

"They're not Mother's parents."

"If they aren't my great grandparents, who are they? Granny is always with them."

"I can't remember their names. But Mother always stayed with them when she had one of her spells. It's one of the reasons I never got along well with my brothers and sister. I had to look after them when Mother was gone. I had to make them mind or she would be angry with me. I'd rather have the children mad at me than Mother."

I asked Mom about Granny's spells but all she would say was, "I think maybe she had high blood pressure. We didn't know much about that sort of thing in those days."

So this couple did not help with the care of the family, they helped Granny while Mom looked after the children. One time when Joyce visited, she said, "Your mom sure was bossy when we were growing up."

Mom said to me, "I never got along well with Joyce, not for years and years, not until we got older and then we got along better and better."

While Mom was helping Granny, Grandad was working to provide for his family. He proofread for the Calgary Herald, and, according to Joyce, he started the first union for newspaper workers in Calgary, very much against management's wishes.

One afternoon when Mom and I sat in the doctor's clinic waiting for her semi-annual visit to have her ears cleaned, she commented, "You see a lot of men with their children these days. You sure wouldn't have seen your dad in here with any of you when you were young. Nor Father, when we were growing up."

"Yes, men help a lot these days," I said. "They change diapers, grocery shop, make meals, do laundry."

"Your dad was never comfortable holding a baby let alone changing a diaper. He never changed a diaper, ever. I don't imagine my father did, either."

"Even when I had my children in the sixties, I never had any help with dirty diapers or daily chores. Shirley gets lots of help from Mario."

"That's good. It's such a big job all by yourself."

All by yourself. Granny had five babies in nine years. Mom had five babies in nine years. Why didn't Granny help, knowing what a big job it was caring for babies all by herself? In the papers in my trunk there are three St. John Ambulance Association certificates awarded to Granny, Mrs. Florence M. Thornton. The first certificate, First Aid to the Injured, is dated March 1928. The course of instruction was held under the auspices of The Alberta Provincial Council, at Calgary and the certificate has a circular legal seal imprinted The General Council Canadian Branch, St. John Ambulance Assn. Inc. 1914. The second certificate is for a Re-examination for First Aid to the Injured and dated November 1939. The third certificate, dated May 12, 1941, also has the official seal of The St. John Ambulance Association, but this certificate was awarded in Home Nursing.

In March of 1928, Mom was nineteen. Her youngest sibling, Johnny, had turned ten in January. While Granny was receiving instruction and studying to qualify to give First Aid to the Injured, Mom looked after the children. In the summer of 1930, Granny travelled by herself to England. Mom again looked after her siblings. In November of 1939, Granny was a certified pupil who was Re-examined for First Aid to the Injured and satisfied the Medical Examiner. At that time, Mom had two little children and was pregnant with a third. In May of 1941, when Granny had taken instruction in Home Nursing, and having been examined was found proficient in the said subject, Mom had three little children, one who wouldn't be a year old until the end of July. Why didn't Granny help with Mom's babies when she had experience and extra qualifications?

I think Granny did help after Mom's babies were born but not in the traditional way of physically being present to walk a fussy baby in the wee hours of the morning so the parents could get some sleep, to take preschoolers for a walk so Mom could nap while the baby slept, to make meals and clean up for a week or two until Mom's body recovered. Mom did this for me and I did it for my daughter. Granny's help came in a different form. Maybe she didn't help with the grunt work, but her moral support provided Mom with the strength necessary to do the daily routines involved with raising children. She also set an example by continuing her education and following her interests long before the women's liberation movement started in the sixties. She did this in the days when women had no rights, and in a setting where her husband ruled the home. Grandad was a hard working and talented man but he was also a reformed alcoholic who grew up in Victorian England. He stood for no nonsense from his wife or children. For them to stand up to his authority would have been a challenge. But Granny managed to study and follow her interests outside of the home.

All of their children received high school diplomas. After graduation, Joyce became a registered nurse. Will entered the military and was a Regimental Sergeant Major during World War Two. Bob and John, after they returned from the war, went to university. Bob received a degree in education. John received his degree in agriculture. Mom followed her love of music and became a certified music teacher, awarded from The Royal Academy of Music in 1930, the same year that Granny travelled to England. Mom minded her siblings while Granny was away, but she also lived her life. She met Dad before 1930 when she was working as a secretary for the same dairy where Dad worked. I found a letter addressed to Miss Dorothy Thornton from Hornsey, N8, London, England postmarked 5 Aug. 1930. Granny wrote, *I am really writing to you about Daddy's letter to me, concerning you and Ole, as you see, you could not continue just the way you were, we have talked things over, and it has been much the same as Daddy has said to you, therefore Dorothy I really am not going to add or repeat anything that has been said; this time that you are passing through, comes to nearly everyone at some time or the other, with some there is no question about it, and a decision can be reached at once, with you there are certain considerations and complications, this is most important, as your whole life is to be affected by them.*

I can only ask you Dearie to think as you have never thought before, to pray for guidance until that guidance and certainty shall come, to wrestle with God as I did; as Abram did, and you will always be sane and certain as I was, and have no regrets and much happiness as Daddy and I have. I know this is your earnest desire, and perhaps you think Ole is the one, Daddy has explained to you why he may not be, the one, and I can only second what he has said. Above all do not hurry, get that holiday with Daddy, tell Auntie Alma if you care to, but I shall be glad to hear from you, when you have time.

It seems as if Ole has been open with you, has written to his own people, but the very person he has overlooked, and should have spoken to, even before he asked you, he has not approached at all, I am very sorry indeed, about this, and I think at the earliest possible time Ole should come and talk over with Daddy all his hopes and ambitions, I guess he is nervous, and a little fearful of doing this, but I know from Daddy he feels it very keenly, and has been slighted when he should have been the first one to be consulted, so I ask you Dorothy, that instead of going for a ride one evening, for you and Ole to take Daddy with you, where you can talk undisturbed or at home. I suggest the ride because it may be easier to arrange and to talk, just take Daddy.

Now I must close, I sent a cable when I arrived, did you get it, it has not been mentioned. Love to you Dearie, from Mother.

Granny writes again, August 21, Thursday, from Hornsey N8 London, England,

Dear Dorothy,

You will perhaps wonder if I am going to answer any of the letters, well I am making a start. Thank you, ever so much for your letter, I can quite understand how you feel, isn't it wonderful. I could say a lot but think I will wait until I see you. I am glad that Ole has spoken to Daddy, he feels ever so much better, by the letter I had from him yesterday, I just love his bulletins, he gave me all the latest news and I felt so well posted up.

Further on in the letter, she writes, *When I do reach home you may have to tie me there, as I have no abiding place here, and I have got the habit of moving on. I am sure you will have to anchor me. I have not had one headache since the train. Everybody is just giving me the loveliest time, this holiday is all we hoped for, in every way. I am writing this in bed, at 8am and must finish.*

The girls are dressing, will write to you all in turn so goodbye Dearie, with ever so much love to you all from your own Mother.

P.S. Had two letters from Daddy this week, hooray for our side.

—

Mom and Dad were married September 24, 1932. Mom told me their wedding was postponed a year due to health reasons. She said that her father built her a special room with lots of windows so she could rest but still get plenty of sunshine. She said she had a spot on her lungs.

A half century later, when her brother Bob visited us in Prince Rupert, he was looking at the family photographs covering Mom and Dad's bedroom walls. A large 16" x 20" black and white print of Mom and Dad hung over the bed. It's a happy photo. Mom is laughing and Dad is smiling at her. When Bob saw the photo, he said, "Oh, Dorothy, I remember that photo. It was taken before you and Ole were married. It was after you had that nervous breakdown."

"That's right," said Mom. "Lunch is ready. Come and get it."

—

In the winter of 1959 – 1960, when Mom was fifty, she started taking organ lessons at the United Church in Nelson. I was fifteen and Mom and I weren't getting along very well. I didn't want to go to Canadian Girls in Training anymore but Mom told me that if I quit C.G.I.T. I would not be allowed to go to Dance Club. I wrote in my diary, "I HATE MY MOTHER!" Dance Club was important to me. With boys lined up on one side of the school gymnasium and girls on the other, we met in the middle, paired up and learned how to waltz, jive, polka, tango and square dance. I never had to worry about being asked to dance at Dance Club. We were there to learn how to dance and everyone had a partner even if it was one of the teachers. Mom insisted I walk directly home after Dance Club and I was in a lot of trouble if I followed the rest of the gang to the Green Door for cherry cokes. I avoided being in trouble with Mom in my teenage years. My brothers and I talk about it every now and then, how Mom could make us mind without ever laying a hand on us. We were scared of her. Her discipline came in a form of disapproval and disappointment. "You know better than that!" Her word was law. I knew I had to go to C.G.I.T. if I wanted to go to Dance Club.

Mom's mid-life infatuation with the pipe organ grew into a life-long love affair. She walked to church most afternoons to practice. Often I walked from high school to church and lay on a pew and listened. Her love of music mingled with her budding love for the organ and resounded throughout high ceilings and stained glass windows, spilling out onto the sidewalk. I knew she was practicing as I walked towards the church.

She became the organist for the church. She led the senior choir and started a junior choir. Sunday services, weddings, funerals and choir practices took an increasing amount of her time and she loved every second of it. One by one her children left home for university or travel, and the responsibilities of motherhood and the burden of household chores lessened. By the fall of 1962 she had an empty nest.

Dad had never allowed her to teach piano after they were married. He said it was up to him to earn the living. He had total control of the purse strings. But there was no income from the organ, and any money that was given for playing for weddings or funerals, she turned over to the church. He was not happy about the amount of time involved, and he grumbled plenty, but he could not stop this addiction to the organ.

Mom's life had a new focus. She rushed home to make supper every night, often rushing away again as soon as the kitchen was cleaned up. When she was short of time she left dishes soaking in the sink. This was the woman who had always insisted dishes must be done and beds made before she left the house.

She continued to care for her parents who were becoming frailer with each passing year. Journal entries in her Five Year Diaries were short and to the point, but Granny was mentioned more frequently in the fall of 1964. Aside from writing, "Played scrabble with Mother after supper," or "Took Mother shopping," Mom also writes, "Mother lost direction from church." "Mother mixed up." "Could not find Mother for supper – up to hospital twice." "Mother did not call today." "Supper at the folks – Mother not going to be bullied." "Bank says Mother cashed in Gov't Bonds – P/A for her (?)." "At the folks for TV – Mother sorting out cards and envelopes." "Mother giving purses away again." "Mother's agitated."

Life took an abrupt change for Mom and Dad early in 1965. The co-operative dairy that Dad managed for years in Nelson sold out and at 59 Dad was unemployed. He accepted a job with Fraser Valley Milk Producers in Prince Rupert and moved north immediately to start work. Mom was left with the heart-wrenching job of dismantling home, severing friendships and commitments to the community, leaving her deeply entrenched affair with the organ and uprooting her aging parents with whom she had spent a lifetime. She told me many times years later that she never forgave herself for abandoning her parents.

Vince and Carol, who were living in Kelowna at the time, found a senior's home for Granny and Grandad in Kelowna and went to Nelson to help Mom sort through and distribute her parent's belongings and to sell their home. Vince and Carol returned to Kelowna with their grandparents and settled them into their new accommodation. Granny's confusion intensified, despite the care and family setting Vince and Carol provided. Granny started hitting Grandad. She was convinced that Grandad was cheating on her, that he was going to marry a younger woman, and she beat him up. By the end of May they were moved into separate accommodation and not long after that Granny was moved to a special home in Vernon. She had totally lost her grasp on reality and lived in her own world. She did not recognize family any longer.

Grandad's health had been diminishing even before the move to Kelowna. He suffered several small strokes over several years that incapacitated him in small ways. His speech was slurred and he had difficulty trying to say what he wanted to say. Granny had been frustrated with him for a long time. When he tried to talk, she yelled at him, "Spit it out! Spit it out!" In Kelowna he did not defend himself against Granny's abuse.

On his own he did not do well. Strokes attacked his body leaving him paralyzed and unable to care for himself. His daughter, Joyce, had him moved to a small hospital in Alberta where she was nursing so she could care for him. It was a sad ending to a teenage romance. I grew up with my grandparents involved in my life. My memories are of them holding hands and laughing and playing together well into their senior years, of their home with the cuckoo clock and bookcases with sliding glass doors, and Grandad making tea and Granny setting out the fancy cups and saucers. When I whistled, Granny teased, "Whistling women and cackling hens are neither good for mice nor men." They were always good to me and I loved them dearly.

—

I lived in Edmonton when I was pregnant with Shirley. One early spring Sunday morning in 1967, I drove south to the small hospital where Grandad lived. He was lying in a bed that held him in like a crib. He was a withered old man unable to do anything for himself. He tried hard to talk to me but no words came. He cried when I said goodbye and my last image of him is in tears reaching out for me with one weak shaking arm. When I got outside I vomited into a snow bank.

Grandad died September 7, 1967. Shirley was born six weeks early, the morning of September 18, 1967 and spent the first three weeks of her life in an incubator. Granny died September 21, 1967. Mom said her final goodbyes to her parents after they were gone.

When Shirley came home from the hospital I phoned Mom and asked if she could come and help me. She was on the next bus.

—

After Mom's major stroke when she was eighty, she was in the hospital for six months. I returned from my winter travels and found the basement in her house overrun with mice. She had opened a twenty-pound sack of flour before her stroke and once her house was vacant, mice made a comfortable nest in the flour to raise generations of mice. Female mice produce litters of four to eight young after a gestation period of three weeks; under favourable conditions they breed throughout the year. The young mature within two months. In addition to the flour there was plenty of other food for the mothers to feed their young. Mom had always planted a vegetable garden in her back yard and potatoes, carrots and turnips were spread out on cardboard to dry. Apples filled a box in the root cellar. Extra boxes of food lined shelves in this cool room.

I don't know how many mice lived in Mom's basement but when three traps were emptied morning, noon and night, it still took many weeks to kill them all. My dreams were filled with mice and the dreams turned to nightmares. I cannot remember any job that was harder than ridding Mom's house of mice.

—

Mom and I laughed when we recalled her helping me in Eckville after the birth of Clint. "I couldn't believe how brazen the mice were," she said. "I remember they ran into the middle of the kitchen floor and stopped and squealed at me while I was setting the traps."

"I don't know what I would have done if you hadn't been there."

"Oh, you would have managed," she said. "We always manage somehow."

Photographs

Dorothy Thornton and her brother Will in Calgary, 1913.

The Thornton children – Bob, John, Dorothy, Joyce and Will at Bowness Park in Calgary, 1922.

Bob, Joyce, Dorothy, John, and Will with their parents, Florence (Granny) and Robert (Grandad), in front of their Calgary home in 1929.

The young Ole Borch before emigrating to Canada.

Ole (standing) with his brother, sisters-in-law, mother and father at their home in Copenhagen, 1922.

Ole hamming it up with Dorothy in 1932.

Dorothy and Ole were married in Calgary September 24, 1932. From left to right, Granny, Bob Thornton, Dorothy, Ole, Will Thornton and Grandad.

Ole and Dorothy's children in Nelson in 1948. From left to right: Dave, Vince, Nancy, Gerry and Mike.

The children in 1998 at a family wedding in Vancouver. From left to right: Mike, Dave, Nancy, Vince, and Gerry.

Grandad and Granny in Nelson, 1964.

Ole and Dorothy in Nelson, 1959.

Nancy, Dorothy, and Shirley at Dorothy and Ole's 50th wedding anniversary, 1982.

Shirley, 20, and Dorothy in Prince Rupert in 1987.

Ole, 1985 and Dorothy, 1986 in Prince Rupert.

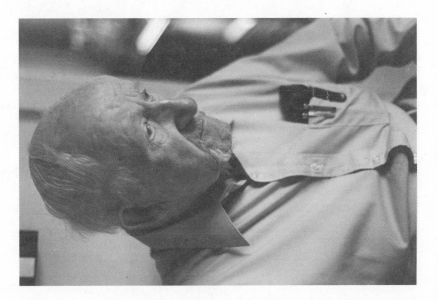

Nancy, a self-portrait, 1987.

Bill in Baja, 1988.

*Shirley, her
husband
Mario, children
Daniel, Allison,
and Michael,
and dog, Levi,
in Kaledon,
2005.*

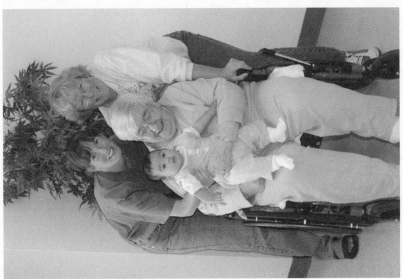

*Shirley May,
Allison May,
Dorothy May
and Nancy May,
2001, in the
Prince Rupert
Regional Hospital
on the fourth floor
extended care
unit.*

Clint and Katherine, 2005 in Richmond.

Nancy and Clint painted these two paintings on a Skeena River outing in 2006.

Dorothy and her sister Joyce celebrate a family birthday in 1994.

Dorothy taking her exercise on the ramp at 1019 Ninth Avenue East in Prince Rupert, 1991.

Dorothy on her 92nd birthday, November 23, 2001, at the Prince Rupert Regional Hospital. This is the last picture Nancy took of her mother.

Abiding places

"W"e're having trouble with some of the inmates," Mom said. She was sitting in her new blue wheelchair with its two-inch thick foam pad. She had already bashed paint off walls and doorways in her small room in The Manor with Dad's old wheelchair before she outgrew it and needed the new, larger one. It was interesting watching her maneuver the lighter, easier to manipulate wheelchair, spinning and turning effortlessly. When she used Dad's chair she had to back up, go forward, back up, go forward to work her way through doorways. Something like watching Dad parallel park before he gave up his driver's license – hitting the bumper on the car behind him then turning the steering wheel and driving forward till he hit the bumper on the car in front of him. He bumped back and forth until he had the car tucked in against the curb.

"What's happening?" I asked.

"One of the men took all of his clothes off in the middle of the hallway. There he was, without a stitch on. Stark naked. His clothes were strewn all over the place."

"What did you do?"

A smile spread across her flushed cheeks. "Well, I wasn't going to bother with him, that's for sure!"

We laughed and I wanted to tease her, to ask, "Why didn't you invite him in? He was ready!" But I hesitated. Telling off-colour jokes or swearing was not part of our relationship. It had never been allowed. "There is no need for that kind of talk," and the clicking of her tongue, the pursing of her lips and the furrowing of her brow left no doubt about the acceptability of such behaviour. But still I hesitated. She had mellowed over the years and now I thought she might like to be teased, to have a little fun and have a little sexy talk. But my conditioned response was to keep my mouth shut.

"You know, he looked sort of ridiculous standing there, exposing himself for the whole world to see. I don't know what gets over some of these people sometimes."

"Are you all right?"

"Of course I'm all right. I wouldn't let something like that upset me. I just turned around and went the other way. I wasn't going to be late for dinner. I stopped at the desk and told them there was trouble in the hallway. Somebody must have done something because he was gone when I came back to my room."

I thought how well she had adjusted to this new life, this ease of living. It was like a reward after a lifetime of hard work. No cooking, no cleaning, no chores, no duties. Just doing whatever pleased her. She had no problem saying, "No, thank you," to anything she didn't want to do. Staff tried to get her involved with crafts and card games but after a brief introduction to group activities, she chose not to participate. She enjoyed exercise class and went willingly. She kicked or lunged at a ball that was tossed around a circle of wheelchair participants. She went to monthly birthday parties and played bingo for an hour before the cake, cookies and tea were served. But she did not want to play bingo any other time. She took part in outings provided by the nursing home: lunch downtown, trips to the mall, picnics, rides around town. She did not need to be reminded to go to the Saturday morning church service. Each week a different denomination led the service. She liked it best when her church, the United Church, was in attendance. She was familiar with the format and hymns. Some of the others seemed a bit odd to her.

"I don't understand all the wailing that goes on and the singing is different. But it's O.K., I guess. It'll do."

Every second Thursday afternoon she attended Bible Study Class. She never forgot to go to this group activity. She found a friend in the group and it brought her pleasure to be with Hazel. Their interests were similar and they were both wheelchair bound. They sat together for meals and the monthly birthday party. When they met or passed in the hallway they reached out to one another and clasped hands. But for most of the day, every day, Mom stayed in her room. She liked her privacy. She preferred to read romantic novels or look out the window rather than see the aging and disabilities of other residents.

Her meals were prepared for her. All she had to do was wheel to the dining room. Because she continued to gain weight, she had been asked to wheel the long way around to get more exercise. The Manor was built in a circle with a hallway separating rooms with a view that faced out, and rooms that faced in, overlooking the courtyard.

Mom had an outside room with a southwesterly view overlooking the mountains and stretching a hundred and eighty degrees to include the harbour. She could watch the sun move across the sky and sink into the Pacific Ocean. She had the full glory of sunsets or approaching storms. She knew what massive cloud formations misted trees along the mountain or threw sheets of rain against rooftops. She watched wind rattle garbage cans down pavement and lift shingles off apartment building roofs.

From her room with a view she could look out and watch the pattern of the neighbourhood. She knew who cut their grass, what day was garbage day, when the old couple walked their dog, where the bus stopped along Summit Avenue. She watched young children dawdle to school in the morning and watched them run, jump and skip their way home after school. She watched teenagers, with backpacks bulging, scurry past the youngsters. "They have something to do, someplace to go," she said. "They are probably going to a music lesson or a part-time job."

She watched teenagers who loitered, bumped one another off sidewalks, pestered the loners and travelled in groups. "They have too much time on their hands," she said. "They are only going to get into trouble."

This small room became her home. Plants lined the window ledge and she watered them with a paper cup that she filled from the sink across from the bathroom. She had a chest of drawers and a desk that held her small television set and her combination radio/ tape deck. A single bed completed the furnishing. She didn't want anything more when she moved in.

"I'll bring some of your things, Mom, and we'll make it cozy for you."

"This will be fine, dearie. I don't want anything else."

"People will think I'm not looking after you if I leave it like this."

"I don't care," she said. "Don't worry what people think."

"Well, I care. I want to be comfortable when I come to see you. I don't want to sit on the edge of the bed."

"Suit yourself, then."

So I did. I took the small armchair, which had sat in Mom and Dad's living room all their married years, to be resprung and reupholstered. The owner of the shop recognized the chair was an antique and suggested keeping the antique look.

"Fine," I said. "Do what you think is best. But I want the material to be blue." The chair had always been covered with royal blue material. When the chair was ready and I went to pick it up, I couldn't believe my eyes. It was beautiful. It didn't look like the same chair I had taken into the shop. There were no springs hanging down and the dark material was gone. It was covered with a pale blue material that had light pink flecks patterned about an inch apart. Two thin coils of the material ran alongside the curved wood on the back of the chair and antique tacks held the material snug next to the curved wooden arm rests and legs.

"That looks wonderful!" exclaimed Mom when I brought the chair into her room. "Thank you."

The next day I brought her long-stemmed trilight, an antique table and some paintings and photographs for her walls. "I don't want all that old stuff on my walls," she complained.

"How about something new?"

"We'll see," she answered.

When I brought two large, framed prints, one by Emily Carr and the other by Tom Thompson, and hung them, she said, "Those look very nice. I like them. That'll be fine."

I hung two enlarged black and white photographs over her bed. One was a multiple exposure of hands on piano keys that my brother, Gerry, had taken and given to Mom for her music room many years earlier. The other was a photograph I had taken of Mom playing the pipe organ during a Christmas Eve service at the United Church when she was at full stride in her music career.

I hung two, small, Danish oil paintings over her desk. I wanted a reminder of my childhood home on her walls. "Now that's enough. I don't want any more," she insisted. It was enough. Enough to keep the room simple but make it cozy.

My sister-in-law, Carol, phoned and asked what she could do to help with the move. I suggested she buy blue drapes for the large window to replace the thin and faded orange curtains that hung limply from the rod. The lined drapes she sent made the room look like a living room. Included in the parcel was a paisley blue curtain to hang across the opening to the bathroom.

My daughter, Shirley, made her grandma a log cabin quilt for a housewarming gift. The colours Shirley chose were blue, different shades of browns, a light beige material with small musical notes, and a gentle shade of red. With the bed being the main focus in a nursing home room, she wanted her grandma to have something special for that area. I wasn't with Mom when the package arrived but Theresa, the attendant who helped her open it, told me later that Mom wept when she saw her gift. That she was overcome with emotion when the quilt replaced the bland bedspread.

I brought an old bookcase that had a dark, wood grain finish and was latticed on the sides. It was another piece of furniture that had always been part of Mom's home. I brought a few of her doilies and knick-knacks to put on the bookcase shelves and desktop; her porcelain shoe collection, a figurine of a mother/father/child in their old fashioned clothes, candlestick holders of two girls with long skirts and bonnets holding baskets that had been a gift from Dad's Danish family, Mom's metal napkin holder that had a picture of Longfellow's home embedded in it. She told me it was a birth present given to her by her mother's closest friend. I brought her Bible, some romance pocketbooks, and a new, blue telephone. I programmed the telephone with numbers of all her children and those of her friends, Helen and Fran, so she just had to press one button if she wanted to call any of us.

I arranged her belongings on the shelves of the bookcase and the desktop. "Thank you, dearie, the room looks lovely. It's very nice to have some of my things around me. Mother brought two of those old shoes and the figurine with her from England when she crossed over to Canada at the turn of the century. All she had with her was what she could put in her metal trunk. What happened to her old trunk? It was in the basement."

"Vince and Carol have it," I answered. "I filled it with scores of your music and shipped it south with the rest of your belongings."

Mom was eighty-seven when she made the decision she could no longer manage living on her own. Although I agreed with her totally, the decision upset me. It was difficult for me to think of separating

Mom from her lifetime accumulation of belongings. It was difficult for me to part with physical possessions that had built my memories of childhood, family and home.

"Don't you worry about a thing," she said. "Everything will work out fine."

She was right. Eventually everything did work out fine. But not before I suffered the separation of Mom from her home, me from her belongings, and gained the knowledge that memories stay intact without having to see and touch.

The hardest part of moving Mom was waiting for a room at The Manor. The waiting list was long. Once Mom decided she did not want to be alone she couldn't understand the delay. She had worked hard to maintain her independence. Now she didn't want it anymore. She lost her will and strength to carry on the daily struggle. She fell often and became easily confused. When she was assessed for level of care, whether intermediate or extended, she could count and spell perfectly. But she couldn't remember where she lived. When asked, she answered, Nelson. Mom and Dad had moved from Nelson thirty years earlier. When asked her address, she answered 205 Second Street, our address in Nelson. When asked her phone number, she replied 565R, the Nelson number.

She was getting frailer as the days turned into weeks and the weeks slipped into months. I was desperately trying to get her into The Manor before she ended up in a hospital bed with broken bones. She was having difficulty transferring herself in and out of her wheelchair and needed an increasing amount of help.

The crisis arrived one cold, gray day late in November. The phone rang while I was at work. It was Eva, Mom's home support worker, who asked me to come right away. "Your mom is on the floor beside her bed and I can't get her up. She's not making any sense and doesn't know where she is."

"Please stay with her, Eva. I'll be right there."

I phoned Bill and he met me at Mom's house. "What's all the fuss about?" Mom asked when she saw us. "Just help me up. I need to go to the bathroom."

She was like a rag doll but Bill got her into her wheelchair and into the bathroom. We sat her on the toilet seat, the special one we had installed years earlier that was elevated and had bars like the arms on a chair. "Now leave me alone," she ordered. "I've got business to do."

"Call me when you're finished," I said.

We were sitting in the living room when we heard the crash. She had tried to stand up and transfer herself to her wheelchair. She had fallen and landed in the space between the toilet and the bathtub. She was wedged in and confused. "What am I doing here?"

We got her out and back into her wheelchair. Her strength was gone. She could not even lift her arms. Her will was gone. She did not protest when Bill wheeled her down the ramp, lifted her into the front seat of the car and drove her to the hospital.

She lay on a bed in Emergency after having her hips, legs and arms x-rayed. Her skin was puffy and red but she did not appear to be in pain when examined by the emergency doctor. He asked her questions. When she tried to answer, only a slight sound escaped her lips and we couldn't understand what she was trying to say. When he lifted her arms and told her to push against his arms, her arms flopped back onto her belly.

She was at the end of the days when she could manage by herself. She did not say, "Leave me be. I want to go home." She lay dazed on a bed in the Emergency Ward.

She never returned to the little wartime house on Ninth Avenue that had been her abiding place for so many years.

—

When Mom and Dad moved to Prince Rupert early in 1965, Mom was immobilized after leaving her parents and her Nelson home. I was living in Vancouver at the time, sharing an apartment in the West End with Judy, a girlfriend I'd met in Whitehorse. We were both broke and struggled to pay the rent every month. When Dad phoned me and asked if I would consider moving to Prince Rupert, that he was worried about Mom, I didn't hesitate. Another friend from Whitehorse, who was sleeping on the couch in our one bedroom apartment, agreed to take over my half of the rent. I booked a stateroom on the Northland

Prince and set sail late one drizzly evening in February. I had recently turned twenty-one.

Mom and Dad met my ferry at the Northland Dock along the bustling waterfront in Prince Rupert. The town was thriving with fishing, logging and construction of a major addition to the pulp mill. I started work immediately for the bank that had transferred me from Vancouver. Dad was busy at his new job with Dairyland.

Mom did nothing amidst all the activity in this flourishing coastal community. It startled me to see her sit and do nothing day after day. She was very quiet. She didn't talk or laugh or nag or bicker. Furniture was still where the movers put it. Boxes remained unpacked. The cover over the piano keys stayed closed. No tantalizing aromas drifted out of the oven. After having his lunch and supper prepared for him every day for thirty-three years, now Dad came home to an empty, cold kitchen.

In an effort to lift Mom's spirits, Dad and I tried to be cheerful and helpful. We grocery shopped and cooked meals. While Mom sat by herself in the living room, Dad peeled potatoes and set the dining room table while I overcooked meat and vegetables. Neither one of us had ever had to be domestic, or responsible for the health of others. Both of us were the youngest children in our families and had avoided the maturity that often comes to older siblings. We had been spoiled and catered to for most of our lives. We had never looked after routines that kept a household running smoothly. But we knew Mom was unhappy so we did everything we could to ease her misery. We scrubbed the toilet and washed floors. We did laundry and ironed clothes. We took turns with the dishes. One night I washed and Dad dried. The next night Dad washed and I dried. It was companionable and pleasant for us to be spending time together but in the back of our minds, we were doing it for Mom. We staggered our lunch hours so she would not be alone quite so long during the workweek. In the evenings Dad did not bury his head in newspapers or stare at TV. He asked Mom if she would like to play a game. Chinese Checkers? Crib? Scrabble? Mom shook her head. So he asked me. It was difficult for me to stay home after living on my own for two and a half years and partying endlessly. But there I was, sitting opposite Dad at the dining room table, hopping marbles across the wooden Chinese Checkers board Mom's father had made for her.

Other evenings, Dad played the piano. He had taken lessons for many years when he was growing up in Denmark. In my childhood, he seldom played the piano but I loved it when he did. He played with flourish and extravagance, pounding the keys, never stopping to correct a wrong note, never slowing down or quieting down for any composer. Mom might say, "Watch your expression!" to one of her sons who was practicing, but she never said a word to Dad. His total abandonment was his expression. He played from memory and he improvised.

Dad opened boxes of music and filled the space under the piano bench and the shelves inside Mom's music stand with books and sheet music. He found the scores that had travelled across the Atlantic with him when he was sixteen years old and emigrating from Denmark to Canada. He now played *Für Elise* the way Beethoven intended it to be played, not galloping away like a runaway stallion.

On Sunday mornings, after we'd prepared breakfast and done the dishes, Dad and I got ready for church. We asked Mom if she would like to come with us, but she shook her head. Mom's religious faith developed in childhood and had remained constant. She always went to church on Sunday. When we were growing up she insisted her five children go too. We went to Sunday School for an hour in the basement of the church and after that, sat with the congregation for the hour-long service upstairs. It was a boring morning for young children. We were not allowed to fidget or whisper. Dad would tap his feet and ruffle pages in the hymnary but his children had to sit still. During prayers we had to bow our heads but Dad took prayer time as an opportunity to count the people in the pews. He could always tell Mom afterwards how many people were in church. Dad only sang the hymns he liked but the ones he liked he sang with gusto: "WILL YOUR ANCHOR HOLD IN THE STORMS OF LIFE?"

Sunday was a day of worship and a day of rest. We were not allowed to play. Perhaps it was the strictness of Sunday that caused the break from religion for Mom's children in our teenage years. Whatever the reason, none of us followed her faith into adulthood. What we all carried with us was her intense love of music. She had a large library of classical records and the sound of piano, violin, choir and orchestral music filled our home every Sunday afternoon. It was also the day when she sat down on the piano bench, set a score of music in front of her, put her fingers on the keys and played the piano for the love of playing and for the love of music. No work was too difficult. She played all the composer's compositions.

Mom's abandonment of Sunday routines when she moved to Prince Rupert had been Dad's signal that she needed help, the reason he had called me. Dad and I did not go to church for our salvation. We went hoping that our interest would spur her interest.

It was not an unpleasant circumstance. Wooden pews, stained glass windows, huge pipes from the organ, familiar hymns. Dad still tapped his feet and ruffled pages in the hymnary. He still got a count on the attendance during prayers. I suppose what made it feel so odd was that Mom wasn't with us. She hadn't pressured us into going. We had willingly gone to church.

Looking back on it I realize the depth of her depression, but at the time Dad and I thought she missed Nelson, her friends, her church, her activities and most of all, her aging parents. I'm sure Dad and I could have said to her what she would have said to us: "Pull yourself together, now. There's no need to act like that." But we didn't. Instead we made meals, did housework, played games, went to church and Dad played the piano.

I don't know what happened to bring about the change in Mom. Perhaps she gave herself the lecture she would have given us. Perhaps she got tired of watching us fumble the routines. Maybe the strength of her faith in God propelled her out of her depression. I don't know what happened, but one Sunday morning, two months after I moved to town, as Dad and I were getting ready to go to church, Mom said, "Wait a minute. I'll get dressed and come with you." That was it. She never talked about how she felt. We didn't ask any questions. Supper was ready when we got home from work, sheets and towels waved on clotheslines, furniture was rearranged, a garden was planted. It wasn't long before she was caught up in the vitality of the community that was to bring personal satisfaction to her and give a wealth of talent and knowledge to others.

Although I stayed in Prince Rupert long enough to see Mom launch her musical career, I moved on, and did not return to live in Prince Rupert for eight years. Dad, however, never forgot that time when Mom was so low. Throughout their remaining twenty-four years together, while he was still able, he continued to peel potatoes for supper and set the table. He dried dishes and swept crumbs off the kitchen floor.

—

Several years ago, when Mom was still living in her home on Ninth Avenue, I dropped in for a visit one evening when she was reading the obituaries in the local paper. She recognized the name of a woman who had recently died.

"She was only fifty-one," I said.

"Such a shame," Mom said. "Her life was just beginning."

Mom was fifty years old when she started organ lessons in Nelson. The lessons sparked a passion that grew into a career after their move to Prince Rupert when she was fifty-six. There was a frontier atmosphere in this industrious town on the north coast of British Columbia. Abundance of work attracted people from all walks of life. Families moved to town with children of all ages and parents wanted their children to start or continue music lessons.

Mom got busier as word spread that there was a music teacher in town who was qualified to teach the older grades of piano and who could teach theory. There was a continual flow of students through her home every day after school and Saturday mornings. As many pupils as Mom had, she could not keep up with the constant phone calls asking if she would please teach another child.

Dad no longer objected to Mom working and earning money. He did complain, after retiring from Dairyland, about young children. He said he couldn't stand the plunk, plunk, plunk, over and over again. He also complained about Mom's impatience with some of the students. He didn't like her hollering, "NO! NO! NO! NOT LIKE THAT!" So Mom stopped teaching beginners and children who wouldn't practice. The pupils she taught were dedicated to learning and Mom was devoted to teaching them. She readied them for Royal

Conservatory exams and for music festivals. She also taught several adult pupils. Many became good friends and often played duets with Mom when they visited. One of her adult pupils told me years later that the time she took piano lessons from Mom was the happiest of her life.

Mom's immersion in the community started once she set foot inside the United Church. Perhaps it was the sight of the huge pipes spiraling skywards behind the wooden benches of the choir loft or maybe it was the familiarity and strength of her faith, but she was drawn into all aspects of church fellowship. She started junior choirs and helped with Sunday School. She worked tirelessly with women's groups. She helped fix up Facey Hall on the east side of town for daycare and Sunday School. In summer, when several canneries were still operating along the Skeena River, a friend drove her along Cannery Road where she stopped at each cannery and established singsongs for the children of the workers. Week after week, while sockeye salmon were caught and canned, Mom gathered children together and gave them choral instruction. She said the children enjoyed singing so much. She also worried about their safety. Most of the wooden row housing was built on pilings, and the tidal water of the Skeena River rose and fell beneath their homes. On the backside of their one or two-roomed homes ran the railway tracks. She couldn't understand how children could spend their long summer days running along boardwalks and playing in such dangerous conditions without getting hurt. Music was her way of keeping them busy and out of trouble.

Mom's involvement with the church included helping with the organ when the organist was unable to play for Sunday services. Any chance she had, she went to the church to practice. The love affair with the organ that had encompassed her life in Nelson grew deeper as she eased into her senior years. When the organist for the church retired, Mom was given the job. Now her career was in full bloom.

Mom expressed the love and joy she felt for music every Sunday morning, every wedding, every funeral. With the exception of Dad, I thought Mom's one true love was the organ. It was an addiction. She couldn't get enough. She could juggle several activities just to make time to get to the church to practice. Grapefruit might be too dear at fifty-nine cents, but no expense was spared for more new music books for the organ. All the other work she did, including teaching, she did to serve the community. But the organ she did for herself. The monthly cheque she received as church organist she endorsed and gave back to the church. When family visited she would not cancel any service or practice that was already planned at the church. Dad would say, "That damn church!" But he didn't say it very loud. I felt his competition wasn't the church. It was the organ.

When they first moved to Prince Rupert, they rented for a few years. I think in their hearts they thought they would eventually move back to Nelson. But life has a way of making readjustments in the heart. By the time they reached their mid-sixties, life was fulfilling, and thoughts of retirement were not on the horizon. Dad was sixty-seven when a younger man replaced him at the dairy but he continued to work part-time for holiday relief and other circumstances. He was also bookkeeper for four daycare centres and for the Thomas Crosby, the United Church mission boat that serviced communities along the coast. They had good friends and good times in the community and they were busy with activities they enjoyed. When they bought their home on Ninth Avenue, their connection to a new life was firmly established and their hearts were at home, too.

Hundreds of pupils walked up the front steps of 1019 Ninth Avenue East. They opened the front door and stepped into the porch where they hung their coats on the coat rack and slipped out of their shoes. They pushed open the curtained, glass-paneled door that was always slightly ajar and stepped into the living room. They knew to work quietly on their homework while they waited for their lesson.

When the music room door opened, Mom came out with whomever she had just taught and said, "Thank you very much, dearie. We'll see you next week. Don't forget to work on your timing." She would look at the next pupil and say, "Hello, dearie. How did you make out with that new piece?" They disappeared into the music room as the door closed behind them.

Music and children flowed through their home. As the years passed, some pupils carried on to university to obtain music degrees, others studied science or education. When they came back to their hometown for Christmas or summer work, they dropped in to visit Mom who was so proud of her students' accomplishments. The pupils who continued their lives in Prince Rupert visited to show off new babies and toddlers. Mom praised and congratulated the start of a new generation. In time she was teaching the children of her pupils.

While Mom taught in the afternoon, Dad sat in his La-Z-Boy chair in the living room reading or watching television that was barely audible. He wore the suit, shirt and tie that he had put on in the morning after his shave and shower. Every morning he was dressed and out the front door by 10:00. He drove to Macey's for coffee then made his rounds to the daycare centres, the mission boat, the bank, the post office, the stationery store. He paid all the bills for his bookkeeping jobs and for the household expenses personally, dropping in to visit local merchants and businesses. It seemed that between Mom and Dad, they knew everyone in town.

He got home in time to peel the potatoes and set the table for their main meal in the middle of the day. Mom had to be coaxed away from whatever project she'd worked on all morning. She was an avid gardener, and flowers bloomed from early spring to late fall. They worked together in the vegetable garden on weekends. Her routine included laundry and housework, baking and sewing. She did home repairs and upkeep while Dad sat in his suit and tie and held the hammer for her. He drove to town for nails, screws, paint or whatever was necessary for her to complete her project.

They held hands while Mom said grace before their mid-day meal and they relaxed in the living room after they cleaned up the kitchen. It was time they spent together every day. Sometimes Dad napped while Mom knitted or crocheted. It was often the only quiet time they had until late in the evening.

Dad drove Mom back and forth to the church for wedding rehearsals, weddings, funerals, memorials, choir practice, church services and Mom's private time to practice on the organ. He was not only Mom's chauffeur, he was also her secretary. While she was busy in the music room, he answered the phone, took messages, made appointments. He never interrupted her while she was teaching. At 5:30 he got up from his chair, went into the kitchen, set the table and put the meal on the table so Mom could eat as soon as she finished teaching at 6:00. Usually she was in a rush to get to the church by 7:00.

All through her sixties and seventies, Mom's life flowed in and out of Ninth Avenue. When Dad started to fail in the mid-1980s, Mom continued teaching in her home but eased up on activities in the church. She gave organ lessons to Judy Rea, a member of the congregation, so the church would not be left without an organist. It was a frustrating time for Mom. She was not ready to slow down but her husband of over fifty years was no longer her helpmate. She could not manage everything all by herself. She had never learned to drive and Dad required more and more of her attention.

I had never seen Mom lonely and frail until after Dad died in September of 1989, three days shy of their fifty-seventh wedding anniversary. She didn't want to eat alone. She didn't want to sleep alone. Suddenly she became wobbly and needed a cane. She still had several pupils coming for lessons and that kept her going for a while. But two months after Dad died, and shortly after her eightieth birthday, she suffered a massive stroke. I think she missed Dad so much she wanted to join him.

Many people suggested I should put Mom in The Manor after her stroke. But Mom was not the sort of person you "put" anywhere. She wanted to return to her little house and six months later, after intensive therapy, she did. When September rolled around, the phone started ringing with requests for lessons. For three more years she taught music, mostly theory and piano to students in the advanced grades. She also had four teenaged boys who pulled chairs close to her wheelchair at the kitchen table every Saturday morning. They had formed a rock band and needed theory to help with their compositions. She tutored other teenagers who already had a music teacher but wanted extra instruction before Royal Conservatory exams.

The autumn just before her eighty-fourth birthday she decided she was not going to teach anymore. She said she did not want to start something she wasn't sure she could finish. When I asked if she would teach me to play the piano, she agreed reluctantly and without enthusiasm. "Are you sure you want to do this?" she asked before the first lesson when we were together in the music room. The upright piano her father had given her when she was a child stood against an inside wall. A stool had replaced the piano bench to make room for her wheelchair. Her old-fashioned music stand nestled next to the piano. There were stacks of music books in cupboards, on shelves and in bookcases. Her large record collection filled shelving along the wall opposite the piano. On top of the piano lay the Danish cloth runner that had decorated the top of the piano since I was a child. In the centre of the runner sat the mother/father/child figurine that had travelled across the Atlantic with her mother almost a hundred years earlier. On both sides of the music room door, and on every square inch of wall space, cards and postcards, handicrafts, pictures – all gifts from pupils for almost thirty years – were tacked, stapled, glued, pinned or taped in a mosaic of colour. Gifts that could not be attached to the walls filled every crevice and window ledge. In the window every stained glass piano, musical note and treble clef that had been given to her by young children over the years hung from the curtain rod. Only the top of the piano remained simple and uncluttered. The metronome and her long pointer rested there and shared the place of honour with the figurine.

Although I can't say that taking piano lessons as an adult was the happiest time of my life, I can say that it was one of the happiest times of my life with Mom. When she was eighty-seven and made the decision that she could not manage on her own anymore, decisions had to be made about all of her belongings. The most important decision was what to do with her piano. My friends could not believe that I didn't want it. I said it wasn't that I didn't want the piano; I didn't want the responsibility of the piano. It had to be in a room with a steady temperature. Bill and I were Snowbirds in the winter and I felt leaving the piano unattended in a cool house would be irresponsible. I would feel terrible if the house was broken into while we were away and the piano vandalized. I wrote to my family asking who wanted the piano. Vince phoned immediately and said, "We'll take the piano."

The day the movers came for the piano, I watched as they removed doorframes from the music room, living room and front porch. I watched as they brought piles of padding from the truck and wrapped and belted the piano. I watched them tilt the piano and set it on a dolly. But I escaped to the kitchen when they moved the piano out through the music room door.

When I visit Mom in The Manor, I look through her cassette case and place a tape in her tape deck. I move the antique blue chair next to her wheelchair and we listen to music while we hold hands and look out the window. Bill has screwed small hooks into the top of the window frame and, using his fishing line, has hung her stained glass musical ornaments from the hooks. They dangle in the top half of the large window and catch light and splash colour on the walls around her room.

I ask her as we listen to *The Glenn Gould Legacy*, "Mom, do you miss your piano?"

"No, not really," she replies. "I'm glad Vince and Carol have it. I like to think that it is being used."

"Vince still plays," I say, "and his children and most of his grandchildren have taken piano lessons."

We sit close together watching clouds drift across the vast sky. She squeezes my hand and without changing her gaze says, "If I managed to instill the love of music in my family and pupils, I have completed the work that God chose for me."

An orange in my knapsack

*W*henever I eat an orange I think of my son, Clinton. He loved oranges when he was a child. I think, given a choice, he would have eaten oranges ahead of any other food. He not only loved oranges, he also loved the colour orange. He would pick the orange crayon out of a new package of crayons and draw his stick family members orange and his house orange with orange smoke billowing from the orange chimney. For his birthday he wanted orange icing on his orange birthday cake. When he was twelve years old, I bought him an orange t-shirt in Hawaii with "Hang Loose" on the front. He wore that t-shirt until it was threadbare.

Clinton left home in the fall of 1987 to attend his first year of university in Victoria. That was the first winter of many that Bill and I travelled to southern California and Baja. Every year new adventures became established patterns for future years. On our drive south, we camped overnight at the Orange Grove RV Park outside of Bakersfield, California and picked oranges from trees that surrounded each campsite like a tall hedge. When I squeezed oranges for our juice for breakfast one of us would comment, "Clint would love this REAL orange juice."

In Baja we would buy a fifty-pound sack of oranges for three dollars before driving down a pot-holed road to camp on a beach somewhere in the outback. Many times we never knew where we would sleep the night. But I knew our bed was behind us as our truck and trailer headed into sunshine and cactus covered hills listening to music that Clint had taped for us.

I brought two oranges into the cab of the truck on the days we travelled. During the morning I peeled the oranges and broke them into segments so I could feed Bill from my fingertips while he drove. A piece for him, a piece for me. We never went a travelling day without eating two oranges. We never went a travelling day without remembering Clint and his love of oranges.

We camped on beaches, hiked up mountains, walked sandy coves and scrambled over rocks. We took the big-wheeled motorcycle out of the back of the truck and explored canyons up sandy arroyos and discovered ranches down winding dirt roads. We never left our campsite without our water bottles, a trail mix of nuts, dates, raisins and cheese, and an orange in each of our knapsacks. We never sat under a palm tree, in the shade of a giant rock or on top of a windy mountain without some reference to Clint as we ate our oranges.

On the way north one spring we left the main highway that winds and climbs through Baja and drove east on a washboard road. We bumped slowly along for about fifteen miles until we got to Coco's Corner, then we travelled in a northeasterly direction towards the Sea of Cortez. We ate our oranges and sang along with Elton John and Blue Rodeo. The washboard intensified and Bill drove even slower. We spent the afternoon bobbing up and down like corks in the ocean. As shadows lengthened we knew it was time to find a place to camp for the night. Every time we stopped along the side of the road and walked to a possible campsite out on the desert, we found broomstick holes all over the ground. We didn't know what creatures dug the holes and didn't want to camp with them. When we walked a distance down the road to look along the other side, it was like walking railroad ties as we stepped on the crests of the washboard. It was dusk when we found a gravel pit scooped out of the side of a mountain. We drove in and leveled the trailer just as night settled around us. We lifted our lounge chairs and footstool out of the back of the truck, wrapped ourselves in blankets and stretched out in dark silence with the night sky covering us. After a while Bill got up and turned off the pilot light on the hot water heater. The slight sound interrupted the still, silent night.

Daylight woke us. After breakfast I filled our water bottles and set them on the front seat of the truck along with two oranges. Bill did his usual check under the hood, under the truck, the tires. "Ten thousand moving parts," he said. "I have to make sure they all keep moving."

There is a comfort travelling with the same person for many years. Going to unknown places is an adventure, not a chore, when you know the person with whom you travel. Steadiness of routines, predictability of responses, strength of character. Knowing you can depend on the other person to fill established roles is necessary when you travel in small homes to vast areas of wilderness for long periods of time. Individually, each becomes a cook or mechanic and you know you can trust the other person implicitly to complete their tasks. Together, two people become companions. Two people to share adversity. Two people to share the joy of beauty, the delight of surprise.

When we pulled out of the gravel pit we knew our chores were done but we did not know what awaited us in the days ahead. We did not know that once on the road we would round a corner and look down on Gonzaga Bay, an oval bay with miles of pristine beach, just a few miles away. We did not know that a windstorm would arrive that afternoon, whip miles of sandy beach into frenzy and obliterate sight of anything beyond the fingertips on our outstretched arms. We did not know that November storms had washed out much of the road and all the bridges over arroyos north from Gonzaga Bay to Puertecitos and that wear and weather had dug deep potholes in the road from Puertecitos to San Felipe. We did not know it would take us four days to travel seventy miles.

We faced each hardship together on that trip. We braved the windstorm by inching the truck and trailer off the beach and down the road until we could tuck into the mountain on the north end of the bay. We sat inside reading and playing crib while the fury of wind shook the trailer. We woke to blue skies and silence and a layer of grit that covered every surface inside and outside the truck and trailer. In the days that followed, we repaired roads, went around roads, made new roads. We found rocks, carried rocks, built rock bridges through sandy arroyos.

Damage caused by the November rain was balanced by the beauty the rain created. Mountainsides covered with tall ocotilla blazed red from flowers that enveloped every branch. Pink flowers bloomed on beavertail cacti scattered across the desert. Yellow, purple, red and orange wildflowers carpeted the landscape.

In the turquoise seascape of the Sea of Cortez, whales breached and dolphins played. We watched pelicans glide on the curl of waves as we settled into Happy Hour at the end of the day. Sometimes we camped high on a cliff that overlooked the panorama of ocean and desert. Sometimes we camped on a beach and at night listened to the lap of waves and the puff of whales.

Familiar routines mingled with the adventure of the unknown. As we ate our oranges every day, we commented on how Clint would love to see the colours of the earth as sun and clouds changed tints and hues on land and water.

We made it to San Felipe, then to Mexicali and finally back to the smooth freeways of Southern California. We drove north through the Imperial Valley and stopped at the Imperial Spa at the northern end of the valley, treating ourselves to hookups for water, electricity, cable TV and hot mineral water pools. Bill removed the big-wheeled motorcycle from the back of the truck and we spent days exploring the Chocolate Mountains and Salt Wash. The rain that caused havoc in Baja had soaked the California countryside and the desert in springtime was in full bloom. The wildflowers were so plentiful that people drove hundreds of miles to experience this once-in-a-lifetime phenomenon. They waded waist deep through a maze of wildflowers.

Each day we rode the motorcycle, I carried my knapsack on my back with our trail mix and oranges inside. We explored every canyon and trail and rode the ridges of the mountaintops. We discovered Red Rock Canyon with its spiraling red clay cliffs and then found a trail that took us to the top of the canyon overlooking a whole network of other canyons. We ate our oranges with warm wind blowing our words over Salt Wash. "Wouldn't Clint love this?" I said.

"Eat your heart out, Clint," Bill replied. Our laughter spilled over canyon walls.

For fifteen winters Bill and I travelled while Clint completed his Fine Arts degree, obtained his teaching certificate and started a career as an art teacher. The abstract canvases he painted were big and bold and vivid.

His travels began small. He went on many camping trips with Katherine whom he met in his second year at university. They tented throughout British Columbia and the Rocky Mountains. After teaching a few years they planned a trip to Europe. Clint came back from that trip and said, "Mom, you have to see the galleries in London and Paris. I would love it if we could go together sometime."

He made two more trips to Europe and returned saying, "Everyone should see Paris once in their lifetime. Someday we'll go together."

Bill and I didn't go south one winter. I was on a different journey. I stayed home to be with my mother as she travelled her ninety-fourth year, her final year, and I didn't want her to travel it alone. Clinton and Katherine could not make a summer trip together as Katherine was completing her Masters degree. "Mom," Clint asked, "why don't we take a holiday together and go to London and Paris for ten days?"

He booked our flight, reserved our hotel rooms and made our Eurostar connections for the Chunnel train. We flew from Vancouver the fourth of August and landed at Heathrow Airport at the start of a heat wave. Our adventure began with perspiration running down our cheeks and sweat drenching our clothes. London and Paris set record-breaking temperatures for the next ten days.

It was comfortable travelling with Clint. He has the same steadiness and strength of character that Bill has. I had never travelled with my adult son but I knew I could depend on him and trust him implicitly. Together we became companions. We shared the adversity. We shared the joy.

We forgot about the heat when we spent hours in air-conditioned galleries. Finding an air-conditioned pub after walking miles was sheer delight. The subway was a new experience for me but Clint got us around effortlessly. Everyone on the subway had perspiration dripping on their collars as they read their papers, standing or sitting, in their office suits. Everyone suffered but no one complained.

Our London hotel room was not air-conditioned but we had double doors that opened to a big balcony. In the evening we took our chairs outside and nibbled on trail mix while we drank cold beer. The streets and sidewalks of the city bustled with a cosmopolitan collection of people enjoying the evening air after another scorching day.

It was even hotter in Paris. When we arrived at our hotel we were happy to enter the air-conditioned lobby but we were ecstatic to walk into our air-conditioned room. It was our haven after hours of walking and exploring the old narrow streets of Paris and standing for hours in art galleries. We retreated to our lovely hotel room in the heat of the afternoon and discussed what we had seen and how we felt about it. It was a special time with no distractions or responsibilities.

Breakfast in the Paris hotel was a feast for the eyes. A bowl of fruit greeted us along with yogurt, cheeses, meats, buns and croissants. There was cereal, hard-boiled eggs, juice and milk.

The last morning in Paris I was too full to eat my orange. I asked the waitress if it would be all right to take it with me. "Oui, Madame," she replied.

After packing my suitcase, I threw the orange in my knapsack. We started our journey to Charles de Gaulle Airport. Despite taking the wrong train at a major underground station, we managed to arrive at the airport in plenty of time for our flight back to Canada. As we waited for our plane, I pulled the orange out of my knapsack and handed it to Clint. He peeled it and split it in two. He handed me the bigger half. I was just starting to tell him how Bill and I talked about him when we ate oranges on our travels but I was interrupted by whistles and shouts and police running towards us. "Move back! Move back!" More police in special uniforms ran into the area. Someone had discovered an unattended bag and the bomb squad had arrived.

The moment with the orange was lost. But it's not lost forever. On our future travels together, I know Bill is going to hear the story about the bomb scare in Paris the summer I travelled to Europe with Clint. Bill's going to hear about the heat wave, the underground, the galleries and the pubs. He's going to hear something about my trip with Clint every time I reach in and take an orange from my knapsack.

An education in love

*I*n November of 2004, I attended my eldest brother's seventieth birthday party. In my tribute to Vince, I told a story about him returning home from university for Christmas when I was nine years old. After supper one evening, while Vince sat at the dining room table discussing adult affairs with Mom and Dad and my second eldest brother, Gerry, I was roughhousing like a bear cub with my two youngest brothers, Mike and Dave, on the living room rug. Vince got up from the table, came into the living room, lifted me out of the fray, swatted me on my rear end and said, "You're a girl! Don't ever let me catch you fighting with the boys again!"

"This," I said in my tribute, "was considered my sex education in the fifties." Laughter erupted from the large crowd of family and friends who had gathered for the party.

On my early evening walk under the November full moon my thoughts wandered. For me, walking is a good way to find out what has settled in my mind in the ordinary course of living each day. Often a thought of something current triggers a memory from the past. I thought of Vince's party and smiled when I remembered the line about my sex education in the fifties. The recent memory mingled with an old memory.

I started school in 1950. I skipped grade five so I was ten years old when I started grade six. Mom must have worried about me being younger and less mature than the other children. Before school started in September, she came into my bedroom and closed the door. She sat on the edge of the bed and said she wanted to talk to me. Mom didn't have time to sit around talking in those days. There was a huge garden to harvest, fruit to pick and can, and laundry to wash in a wringer washer, rinse in tubs and hang on the clotheslines. There was ironing, baking, sewing, mending, housework, meals to prepare and afterwards, the cleanup. Always the cleanup, or the supervision of the cleanup. "Pick up your clothes. Make your bed. Don't leave your belongings scattered around. Pick up after yourself." Always the supervision of chores. "Set the table. Do the dishes. Cut the grass. Dig the potatoes. Pick the cherries, don't eat them." Sitting around talking during the day was not a normal occurrence.

When Mom came into my room, I thought I had done something wrong and was about to be lectured. Mom set high standards for behaviour and was not shy about telling me, or my brothers, of her disappointment when her standards weren't met.

I was sitting on the floor playing with my Jane Arden paper doll cutouts that I collected from the Star Weekly. Mom wore a printed cotton housedress covered with a flowered bib apron. It was too hot for her stockings so she rolled them down to her ankles. On her feet she wore sensible oxfords. Her long, graying hair was tucked neatly into a bun at the nape of her neck. When she sat on the bed she patted the silky pink bedspread she had made for me. I got up and sat beside her.

"Nancy," she said, "you are younger than the other children in your class and I don't want you hearing things from them that you don't understand. When you become a woman your body will make an egg and once a month your body will release this egg. Always with this release you will have a lot of blood."

She said she would put pads in my top dresser drawer to prepare me for this coming of age.

I didn't know what she was talking about. I asked, "Is this why my brothers get nose bleeds?"

Mom got up from the bed, crossed to the window and looked out. She didn't make a sound but her shoulders shook. She could not stop smiling. I can imagine her telling Dad about the nosebleeds as they curled up together in their double bed at the end of their long workday. I can imagine their muffled giggles.

However, when I did start my monthly cycle of menstruation, I was not frightened. The message Mom gave me that late summer day registered, and although I did not understand the whole equation, I understood that this bodily function was expected. Many women my age tell stories that they feared they were bleeding to death.

Browsing through Mom's journals after she moved into The Manor, I found a brief entry for January 15, 1956: "Nancy entered womanhood today." If I had not read that I would not know how old I was or what time of year I entered womanhood. It could have been when I waded through waist high snowdrifts on our family search for the perfect Christmas tree. It could have been when creeks ran fast and high under railway trestle bridges that I crawled across on my hands and knees while Mike and Dave skipped from tie to tie. It could have been when I followed my brothers to Lakeside Park and swam in Kootenay Lake to escape the summertime heat. It could have been when autumn painted the town of Nelson and the surrounding mountains gold and orange and I hiked through crispy leaves with Mike and Dave on the trail to Pulpit Rock.

I don't remember when I entered womanhood. I do remember getting menstrual cramps that crippled me. Sometimes I was driven home from school by the school nurse or principal after throwing up or fainting from pain. Mom was not sympathetic. "You are not to treat this as an illness. You are not sick. This is a normal part of life. Now go back to school and pay attention."

She wrote in her journal for January 31, 1957: "David thinks he will have to shave soon."

Dave is seventeen months older than I am. We shared the tub for our Saturday night bath throughout our young childhood. We played with spoons and plastic bowls and washcloths until the bathwater turned cold. When I started school I had to bathe alone. When I started menstruation I was not allowed to have a bath. Mom said it was unsafe to bathe at that time of the month.

As a young child I had to wear the tops and bottoms of my pajamas. The boys went to bed wearing just the bottoms. When the heat of summertime lingered into the evening, I took the top off and climbed under the sheet in just my bottoms. When Mom came to tuck me in and hear my prayer, "Now I lay me down to sleep…" she insisted I put my top back on.

"How come I have to wear my top and the boys don't?"

"Because you're a girl. I don't want to hear any more harping about this."

"How come I have to say my prayers and the boys don't?"

"They do say their prayers. They don't need me to hear them anymore, that's all. Now, no more back talk."

"God bless Mommy, Daddy, Vince, Gerry, Mike, Dave and Granny and Grandad."

"Sleep tight, dearie." She kissed me goodnight and pulled the sheet up around my neck and tucked it around my shoulders.

Mom and Dad always kissed me goodnight. I never outgrew that nightly ritual. When I was a teenager and pushing limits, I knew

I was late if Dad was outside pacing up and down the sidewalk in his pajamas, housecoat and slippers. It embarrassed me to have my friends see him like that. It was the worst possible punishment for being late. He never had to say a word. When we got in the house, he kissed me goodnight and said, "Hurry up, honeybunch, and get to bed."

Mom made me baby doll pajamas for summer. I loved them. Not only were they cooler than my ordinary pajamas, they were pretty and feminine and, although I didn't know the expression then, sexy. I was confined to my bedroom when I wore them. Mom warned, "Don't let me see you prancing around the house like that." None of us pranced around the house in our pajamas anyway. Pajamas were covered with a housecoat outside of the privacy of our bedrooms.

I never saw my father's or brothers' naked bodies except when Dave and I bathed together as pre-schoolers. I had no idea what an adult penis looked like. Even if I'd seen one, I wouldn't have known what it was for except for urinating. When I think back to the fifties, it was a time of ignorance or naiveté, not just about sex education, but knowledge of world affairs too. There was no television, no talk shows. CBC radio had *Saturday Afternoon at the Opera* that Mom listened to each week. *Mockingbird Hill* and *How Much Is That Doggie in the Window* was the type of music played on the radio. I did not know about apartheid in South Africa or wars, famine, droughts or hurricanes in the rest of the world. Aside from the news clip when I went to the Saturday matinée to watch the latest sequel of the western movie, or children's books at the library, knowledge came mainly from school. We learned to read, write, spell, add, subtract. Good penmanship was required as was good grammar. If we were in trouble at school, we were in trouble with Mom at home. "I don't want to hear any back talk. You do as you're told."

In junior high school, a new course was added to our curriculum. Health and Personal Development, or HPD as we called it. Mostly we were taught about personal hygiene. I think it was considered to be our sex education but teachers skirted anything that might be valid or necessary to know about sex. I got the impression we were not supposed to "do it." Whatever "it" was wasn't made clear. I learned I was supposed to be a virgin when I married. That I was supposed to "save myself" for my future husband. I did not learn that boys are horny and would almost always try to "get into my pants." I did not learn about birth control. I did not know what a condom was or what it looked like.

The teacher who taught HPD in grade seven was a middle-aged spinster who wore what the boys called falsies. One of her sharply pointed falsies slipped down on a regular basis, which gave the boys reason to misbehave. Her class was usually out of control, which might be another reason we did not receive any education in sex. I'm sure she was as uncomfortable with the subject as we were. While paper airplanes and erasers flew around the room to rude sounds of hands smacked under armpits and farts and burps that boys seem to be able to produce on demand, she stood helplessly repeating, "Now class. Now class."

I was eleven when I started grade seven in junior high school. Most of the girls were aged twelve to fifteen and wore brassieres. I really wanted to be like the other girls so I asked Mom if I could have a brassiere. She said, "You don't need one."

Although I had never seen an adult naked male body, Mom's body and the clothing she put on it were totally familiar to me. Since my earliest memories, Mom was a part of my every day. She would pair up the boys so they could look after each other, but she took care of me. When we went shopping or to tea at one of the neighbour's, I waited for her and chatted with her in her bedroom while she changed from her everyday clothes to her good clothes. I watched as she put on her undergarments. I knew how she did up her brassiere. How she pulled up her stockings so the seam at the back was straight. How she attached the stockings to her garter belt, or her girdle if it was a special occasion. I watched as she slid her lacy slip over her head and shoulders and smoothed it over her hips. It was a comfortable time with Mom, a time for me alone, a time when I wasn't in trouble for talking too much, jumping on furniture, running in the house, slamming the door, talking with my mouth full, interrupting others, acting silly, forgetting my manners. It was a special time with Mom when I gradually learned about being female without any verbal instruction.

When I started grade eight and again asked for a brassiere, Mom asked, "Is it that important, Nancy?"

"Yes. All the girls wear one," I replied.

We went shopping together and found the smallest cup size that was made so I could dress like the other girls.

Dad shopped for Mom's lingerie. Always on her birthday and for Christmas, he came home with a box from Dee's Ladies Wear. He chose beautiful, silky blouses and lacy slips and nightgowns.

When he came home from work he wrapped his arms around Mom and gave her a noisy kiss on the back of her neck while she stood at the stove putting the finishing touches on supper. She walked to the front door with him when he left for work in the morning and hugged and kissed him before he went out the door. She stood and watched with her arms crossed one over the other until his car disappeared from sight.

Their bedroom was big and roomy and had the only double bed in our old, two-story home. We were not allowed into their room without knocking. On weekend mornings, once Dad was downstairs, I went into their room and crawled into their warm and cozy bed beside Mom. Their sheets, blankets and crocheted bedspread smelled different than the bedding on my bed or my brothers' beds. The fragrance in the room seemed to be part of Mom and Dad and was noticeable even when they were not in the room. Their bedroom was special, filled with love, a love I did not know or understand as a child, but it gave me hope as an adult that I could have such love in my life.

When my children were young, I thought I could give my daughter an education in sex and teach her to be responsible for her own sexuality. But I didn't know how to do the same for my son. When Clint was about five years of age, I asked my brother, Mike, "How old were you when Dad told you the facts of life?"

"He didn't," Mike replied.

"He didn't tell you anything?"

"Nothing."

"He must have told you something," I insisted.

"No, he didn't. He never said a word."

"What about Mom? Did she tell you anything?"

"No. But I know she tried. When I left home she hugged me, then put her hands on my shoulders and said, 'Take good care of yourself, Michael.' The way she said it, and the look in her eyes when she said it, spoke volumes. I've always thought of that as my sex education."

When I was an older teenager Mom gave me one other piece of information for my education in sex. She told me that her father told his three sons that the only sure means of birth control was to "turn your back." That probably wasn't the best advice she could have given me. Perhaps she should have said that to her sons. But she did make an attempt to make me aware of birth control before I left home.

I certainly lacked an education in sex when I started my young adult life. But like most everyone else brought up in the fifties, I eventually figured it out. What I did get was an education in love. Mom and Dad taught us the basics of love and kindness when she ironed his shirts and he polished her shoes. When he drove her to church and she cooked his favourite roast beef dinner. When they hugged and kissed. When they bickered and made up. There was a balance in their marriage. A decency mixed with physical attraction. Their love was expressed daily in their terms of endearment for one another. Sweetheart, honey, dear and darling were sprinkled throughout their conversations.

They might not have told me anything about sex but they certainly showed me the way to find love.

How will it
all turn out?

*F*or some reason I assumed that when Mom was dying she would lie peacefully in a hospital bed and I would sit on a chair beside her bed holding her hand. I thought she would say something like, "Thank you, Nancy. You've been so good to me." Then I thought she would quietly and cooperatively die.

I assumed that because that is the way she lived her life after she turned ninety-one, thanking me every time I read to her or took her for a walk. She sat in her wheelchair beside her hospital bed in extended care day after day, reading or sitting quietly, never complaining, never demanding, waiting for care that she knew would eventually come. She never hollered or banged her hairbrush on the metal rungs of the hospital bed or rang the bedside buzzer for attention.

However, when I got the call, "Can you come right away?" what I discovered in Mom's room was anything but a model dying patient. Here was a woman who had kept the whole ward awake the night before with her constant loud talking and demands to get up and go home.

"Mother! I'm so glad you got here! The boxes are all packed and ready for you." She pointed to the end of her bed, "All that was left to me were two chickens and the henhouse."

So started my bedside vigil. I was her mother, not her daughter, and most of her nonstop gibberish made no sense. "That time in Edmonton was really too bad, wasn't it, Mother?"

"Yes, it was," I agreed, hoping to hear secrets from her first forty years when she lived in Alberta. I had asked lots of questions over the years but Mom deflected them. "Why are you asking these questions?" "How come you want to know that?"

Now I listened to her babble and knew her secrets were safe. Nothing made sense. I couldn't tie anything she talked about to any of the questions I wanted answered.

Two days of feverish ramblings. Laughing and talking with siblings, and with her five children as youngsters. When she heard a baby cry in the hospital hallway, she smiled and said, "Oh, good, the children are here, Mother!" But I didn't know to what generation of children she was referring.

I thought that a person died after they started dying, so I sat with Mom hour after hour so she wouldn't be by herself. Exhaustion set in and eventually I gave in to it. When I got up to leave, Mom cried, "Why are you leaving me? Please take me with you, Mother. Don't leave me here by myself. I don't like it here."

I reassured her, "I'll be right back, Mom. I have to get some sleep."

"Take me with you. I promise I won't be any trouble."

"You're not strong enough to get in and out of the car and I'm not strong enough to lift you. I won't be long, I promise."

Tears ran down her cheeks. Her hands gripped mine. "Please take me with you, Mother. I want to go home."

I sat back down and wiped her tears. "I'll stay a little longer."

A genuine smile filled her face. The gibberish started again and as she talked, her speech was interspersed with laughter. Her animation surprised staff and visitors. They had never seen her act so outrageously and have so much fun.

I thought eventually she would tire and I would slip away for a few hours. But she lasted two days. The second night, she stopped the nonstop babble. She looked me in the eyes and asked, "How will it all turn out?"

"I don't know, Mom."

"It sort of makes you wonder, doesn't it?"

Her eyes closed and her body relaxed. Too tired to leave, I laid my head on her bed beside her body. I felt her hand move. She lifted it and put it on my head. I fell asleep as she gently stroked her fingers through my hair.

I was startled awake by a hand on my shoulder. Doctor Coburn spoke to me, "Go home, Nancy, you're going to wear yourself out."

"I don't want to leave her by herself."

"Come with me. I'll explain what's happened."

We sat together in the silence of the nighttime nursing station. The hallways were dimly lit. Rooms were dark behind doors slightly ajar. I could hear the staff's muffled voices in the coffee room. In a quiet voice Doctor Coburn explained that Mom had had another stroke and her electrolytes were out of balance.

"My experience is that she will probably keep getting little strokes and get weaker and weaker. I think she will slowly go down, down, down." His splayed hands moved in steps down to his knees in demonstration of his words. "There is nothing you can do, Nancy. She is well cared for here. Go home and get some sleep."

I wanted to be strong, mature, capable in front of this man who had cared for Mom for so many years. Even before her massive stroke twelve years earlier, he had cleaned her ears, removed infected toenails, kept her blood pressure under control. He had made house calls to Ninth Avenue to check on her when Bill and I travelled in the winter. She had given his children piano lessons. She called him "Doctor." He called her "Dorothy." She saved her most brilliant smile and sharpest humour for him.

I'm sure he never saw her cry even when she had worked diligently to recover from her stroke. She impressed him and the hospital staff with her determination to talk and walk again. Tears were not an option. "There's no need for tears. That's not going to do anyone any good." I could hear the words she would say to me now if she saw my emotional state. "Come on now, pull yourself together."

I wanted to be strong. I wanted to say, "Thank you, Doctor," but all I could manage was a smile before turning and fleeing down four flights of stairs instead of waiting for the elevator.

—

Two years earlier, when I was advised that Mom would be moved from intermediate care at The Manor to a four-bed ward in extended care at the hospital, I fought the move. Mom seemed perfectly comfortable in her cozy room. She watered her plants and talked on her telephone. She read for hours stooped over in her wheelchair in front of her big window with its vast view of mountain, sky and ocean. She had privacy for family and friends who dropped in often. Everyone was greeted with a big smile and a warm welcome. She was always cheerful, never complaining, always thankful for small mercies.

She wheeled herself to meals and to activities that interested her. She caused no disturbances, demanded nothing. She said, "Thank you," for the slightest care given. The nurse who administered medication was thanked, as was the attendant who helped her on and off the toilet. The kitchen and cleaning staff received gratitude daily.

She appreciated any effort made towards her comfort and no one ever heard her complain.

When Mary, the health care supervisor, phoned to tell me that Mom would be moved to extended care in the hospital as soon as the next bed was available, I was stunned.

"Why Mom?" I asked.

"She's next on the list, Nancy."

"What's that got to do with anything?"

"Would you want me to put someone else's name ahead of your Mom's?"

"Yes, I would."

"I can't do that. It wouldn't be right."

"Why not? Mom's perfectly happy where she is. She's no trouble. She loves having her own room. She loves her privacy. Why not move someone who lies in a bed in the hallway all day? Someone who doesn't want to be alone. There are at least a dozen people sitting around the hallways or beside the front door who don't want their privacy."

"This is not a privacy issue. It is a care issue."

"Well, move someone who can't feed herself anymore. There are a lot of people in The Manor who need more care than Mom."

"I feel terrible that this is upsetting you. I wish I didn't have to do this."

"I don't understand why you would even consider it."

"I have to. Your mom requires more care than she can get in intermediate care. The Manor is designed for people who can basically look after themselves with the help of one attendant. Your mom has gained weight. She's now two hundred and twenty pounds. She needs two people to help her on and off the toilet and to get her in and out of bed. She has slowly been getting weaker and it is time to make the move to extended care while she's well enough to make the adjustment."

"I can't believe Mom takes more care than some of those poor old souls who lie in a reclining chair in the hallway babbling to themselves all day."

"I have to do this, Nancy. I'm sorry I'm the one who has to tell you."

"I'm sorry, too, Mary. I'm sorry that I have to fight you on this. Please give me the phone number of your immediate supervisor."

"I am the one in charge. But this is not one person's decision. I make this decision based on consultation within the system. It is a care issue. I have to be fair to your mom and I have to be fair to caregivers."

"You must answer to someone. I need a phone number of someone higher up the ladder. I don't care if it's the premier of the province. I need to stop this move."

My hands shook as I wrote down the phone number she gave me. My whole body shook. I was so angry the skin on my body flamed. I couldn't believe the days, months, years of peace had to end.

I thought of Mom's time in The Manor as the halcyon years. She was content to leave her life's work behind her. Content to have someone else do the cooking, the cleaning. Content to be finished teaching music. When I asked, "Do you miss your piano?" she answered, "Not really." When friends asked, "Do you miss your home?" she answered, "No. I'm happy here."

When I fought the move, I was fighting for Mom. I didn't want her idyllic lifestyle to come to an end. What I didn't know was that I was fighting for me, too. My life was so simple with Mom safely and happily in The Manor. I walked to visit her every second afternoon. We sat together as we discussed the book she was reading or the project on which I was working. I would put one of her tapes into her tape deck and we sat side by side, holding hands, looking out the window, listening to pianists play Bach, Mozart or Beethoven. Sometimes we listened to one of the many orchestral or choral tapes her son, Gerald, had made for her over the years.

Often I picked her up and took her for a drive. She waited in the car while I ran in and out of the post office or bank. We drove to the recycling centre and out along the highway, sometimes to Oliver Lake, sometimes to Port Edward. We stopped at McDonald's for an ice cream cone on our way back and sat in the parking lot, facing the street and the sidewalk, and watched the world go by. Her comments about weather, about new growth on trees or about leaves almost all gone, were interspersed with, "My, this tastes good."

If I went to the liquor store she did not sit in the car and wait. I got her wheelchair out of the back seat, opened the passenger door and she transferred herself into the chair. Inside the liquor store, I wheeled her around the store. We didn't miss an aisle. She studied the colour and design of bottles and the patterns they formed when stacked on shelves. She was amazed at the huge collection of bottles in one place. "Isn't this something," she repeated every visit.

Bill and I continued to pick her up for Sunday suppers and for special occasions. She anticipated a glass of wine when she arrived and was disappointed if we didn't have any. "Why didn't you tell me? If I'd known you were without wine I'd have bought a bottle when we were out yesterday."

Bill teased her every week. "Do you want a little wine?

"Yes, please. That would be nice."

He poured a drop into her glass. "Is that enough?"

"I want more than that!"

"You said you just wanted a little."

"Well, I want a little more than that!"

After supper, when her normally pale cheeks had a rosy blush, I moved her wheelchair next to the drain board and pushed the table next to her. As Bill washed the dishes, she dried and set them on the table. When they finished I moved the table back and Mom and I played Scrabble while we listened to the classical music of *Sound Advice* on CBC radio.

Sometimes when I picked Mom up, and if the weather was warm, we drove downtown, parked the car and went window-shopping. I wheeled her up one side of Third Avenue and back down the other side. Old friends and music pupils paused to chat. We stopped at City Hall to admire flowers and stopped at Macey's for tea. Sometimes we went to see the exhibition in the museum art gallery. Sometimes we wheeled the paths at the provincial court house to see the gardens. "My, they take good care of the flower beds. It's so nice to see."

It was on one of those Saturday afternoon outings, when there was still some warmth to the autumn sun, that I should have recognized what Mary was eventually going to tell me. Mom was getting weaker. I had been ignoring little signs. She could no longer climb the three steps up to our front porch. Bill had to drag her up while she clung to the sturdy railing he built for her. She plopped her body into her waiting wheelchair, closed her eyes and exclaimed, "Whew! What's the matter with me, anyway?" She couldn't transfer herself from her wheelchair to our toilet, not even with my help.

It was a Saturday afternoon when the end came for our excursions with the car. Mom could not transfer herself from the wheelchair back into the car. We were parked on a side street and I backed the car up to an alley so Mom wouldn't have to step off a curb. I wheeled her chair parallel to the passenger side of the car, opened the door and wound the window down. Mom gripped the window ledge of the car door. When she lifted her body to transfer herself into the car she fell and her body wedged between the chair and the car. I clung to her and pleaded, "Mom, you have to make it. You'll end up on the ground. Push with your legs and pull with your arms."

"I can't, dearie. My legs aren't cooperating."

A pick-up truck drove down the blocked alley. The truck stopped and a young man with shoulder length hair and tattooed arms got out. "What's the matter here? Do you need a hand?"

"Please," I requested. "I'm not strong enough to lift Mom into the car."

Mom's firm grip on the window ledge of the car door had prevented her from falling onto the pavement. The man pushed and lifted Mom's behind. He managed to get her rear end onto the edge of the seat and, in stages, as she lifted with her arms, he pushed until she was fully onto the seat. "Oh," she sighed, "That's better. What can I give you to show my appreciation?"

"You don't have to give me anything," he replied. "I'm glad I could help."

"You're an angel in disguise," I said. "I can't thank you enough."

"No problem," he answered.

"We'll get out of your way," I said as I squeezed the handles on Mom's wheelchair together and tilted it into the back seat of the car. "Sorry to hold you up."

I eased the car forward into our parking space next to the curb. The young man tooted the truck's horn and waved as he roared past.

"I'm sorry, dearie," Mom apologized. "I'm such a nuisance."

"You're not a nuisance, Mom. It was an accident."

"No. No, it wasn't. My legs have been causing me trouble for some time now. They don't want to hold me up anymore. I shouldn't be putting you through all this work. I think we'll have to call it quits with the car. I can't manage it anymore."

I reached over and took her hand. "We'll see," I said.

Mom handled the transitions better than I did. She accepted change and carried on, each step making her life simpler. For me, change meant loss. Although I hired the Handi-Dart bus to take Mom to the doctor or to take us to town, the bus did not operate on weekends or evenings so it meant no more Saturday afternoon outings and no more special occasion or Sunday suppers together. For months I could not listen to *Sound Advice* Sunday evening. I took the Scrabble board and the tobacco can full of letters to The Manor along with the regular dictionary and Scrabble dictionary that Vince and Carol sent one Christmas. But Mom did not want to play Scrabble anymore. "No thanks, dearie. Not today."

Early in December I brought her previous year's Christmas cards, her old address book and a new box of cards to The Manor. "Is this really necessary?" she asked.

"I think so, Mom. Look at all the cards from last year. Almost all of them have letters inside. I'm sure your old friends would love to hear from you."

"Well, if you insist," she said.

We moved into a little room with table and chairs and a view of the inner courtyard. I addressed envelopes while Mom chose what card she wanted sent to whom. Other years she wrote a few lines of greeting. She was specific in signing. "Love from your sister, Dorothy" or "Love from your aunt, Dorothy" or "Love from Grandma Borch." Her five children got, "Love, Mom."

Other years this had been a companionable job. It usually took several afternoons to complete the cards. We talked about her old friends in Nelson and her old friends who had moved from Prince Rupert. We talked about family. "I wonder how Graham's doing," she pondered. Or "Have you heard from David lately?" She talked about music pupils she had taught. How she had enjoyed playing duets with them on the piano or how proud she was of their accomplishments.

But this year was different. She signed every card "Dorothy" and handed it to me. "Is that all?" I asked. "Aren't you going to write a few words?"

"No."

"This one's going to Vince and Carol. I think we should get another card so you can sign it "Mom.""

"Don't worry about it. It'll do."

I should have registered the changes as they occurred, and accepted them, instead of trying to keep old patterns operating. Mom had already celebrated her ninetieth birthday. She was willing to relinquish obligations, competition, pleasure. She wanted to sit and read. She was at peace with her diminishing capacities. I was the one upset by change.

Instead of acceptance, I fought Mary. I fought the person who had helped so much with the care of my parents in their aging years when they lived in their little home on Ninth Avenue. She gave loving and professional care to Mom for at least ten years and helped with Dad for at least five years before that. She went to their home not only in her capacity as a home care nurse but also as a friend. She sat and visited after changing dressings or taking blood pressure readings.

Perhaps one of the reasons for my fight was my trust in Mary. I thought I could make her see how wrong she was. "No," I said to her, "you can't do this to Mom. She is so clear right now. She has a new hearing aid and is so on-the-ball."

Later, when I saw Mary in The Manor, she told me the move had been stalled.

"Oh, thank you," I exclaimed.

"It's still coming. She's still top on the list. I've spoken to your mom. She knows about it and she's fine with it."

When I got to Mom's room she was sitting looking out the window. "Hello, dearie," she said. "Have you talked to Mary?"

"Yes," I answered.

"So you know what's going on?"

"Yes, I do. I'll try to stop the move."

"I don't understand it," she said. "I don't cause any trouble. I don't want to go back to the hospital. That's where I came from."

"Did you tell Mary that?" I asked.

"No. I don't want to cause any trouble."

For two weeks I didn't hear anything so I ignored the situation. But ignoring change didn't prevent it. I returned home one day and there was a message from Mary to call her.

My heart was banging when I returned her call.

"There is a bed available for your mom, Nancy."

"This can't happen."

"Your mom is not unhappy. She's fine with it."

"Mom doesn't want to move. She just doesn't want to cause any trouble."

I was with Mom when Denise came from the library to pick up her old books and drop off four new ones. Mom told Denise that she might have to bring the books to the hospital next time.

"Why?" Denise asked.

"I don't know," replied Mom. "I'm perfectly happy here."

I repeated the conversation to Mary.

"I'll be phoning long distance to your supervisor and I'll be phoning anyone I can think of to stop this move."

"I'm sorry, Nancy. I wouldn't do this if I didn't think it was necessary for the care of your mother."

At the end of the day, despite my desperate fight, the final word was that Mom would be moved to extended care. Mary's supervisor phoned late afternoon. Her voice was firm but kind. "Nancy, your mother will be moved to extended care on the fourth floor of the hospital. We will delay the move until Saturday so that you can pack her belongings and be with her for the move."

I couldn't speak. I had made so many phone calls during the day I had no words left.

"You fought hard, Nancy. You even had the CEO of the hospital and one of the directors checking the fourth floor. You have really stirred things up. I know you don't agree with this decision but I think you will find that this move will be very good for your mother."

Mom accepted the move with grace. She gave instructions Saturday morning while Bill and I packed her belongings into boxes. "I won't need those knick-knacks anymore. You can take them with you."

When we left Mom's room at The Manor she never looked back. The final click of the latch resounded in my heart like the click of the gate the last time I closed it after moving Mom from her home on Ninth Avenue.

As we wheeled down The Manor's hallways, staff came to Mom, hugged her and wished her well. She thanked them and teased, "You be good now. Don't do anything I wouldn't do."

I couldn't speak. The anger embedded in me made me dizzy, nauseous. I thought about my horoscope in The Daily News, "Don't let your emotions spoil what is a perfectly pleasant situation."

I wanted to lash out at staff, "Why didn't you help stop this move? How could you let this happen?" But I kept my mouth shut. I thought of Mom's admonishment when I was a teenager, "If you can't say anything nice, don't say anything at all."

In extended care, the nurse on duty, Sumitra, was waiting for us. She met Mom with a huge smile and a big hug. "Dorothy, we are so happy to have you with us. Do you remember me? I was your neighbour on Ninth Avenue. I lived across the street from you. You taught both of my children how to play the piano."

"Of course I remember you. How are you?"

"I'm fine. Let me show you your new home."

She wheeled Mom down the hallway and showed her the bright kitchen and dining area with the same panoramic view she had from her room in The Manor. She wheeled Mom into a big living room area with its comfortable chairs and couches, television and piano. She showed us a smaller living room for entertaining guests. A place for privacy. Finally she took us to Mom's room. A four-bed ward. "This is your corner, Dorothy. You have your own dresser. There is a closet for you just around the corner. You can use your television if you want. We'll set it up for you."

"No, thank you. That won't be necessary."

"We can bring your small television to you, Mom."

"I said that won't be necessary. I don't want the television. I don't want anything. I'm fine just the way I am."

"O.K., Dorothy," Sumitra said. "The buzzer is here on the bed if you need anything. Just press it and someone will come as soon as they can."

"Thank you very much. I'll be fine."

I stayed with Mom for the afternoon. I folded her clothes and put them in her dresser and hung her coats in the closet. We were both quiet. Mom's new surroundings felt strange. We weren't used to conversing with three sets of eyes on us. It was a long, uncomfortable afternoon. "I can't believe this," I grumbled as I sat on the edge of Mom's bed.

"Get over it, Nancy. Life carries on."

When supper arrived at four-thirty, a tray was brought to Mom and set on her wheeled bedside table. "Let's take your supper to the kitchen, Mom."

"I'm fine right here, dearie."

"No. You can't sit in this corner all day, every day. You can wheel yourself to the kitchen for meals. There's a lovely view from there."

It was the start of a new routine and one that Mom maintained for two years. Staff knew that Mom would be waiting for her meals at a table in the kitchen looking out at storms, sunsets and seasons, and her tray was brought to her where she patiently awaited its arrival.

When I left Mom that day, it felt more like an escape than an abandonment. She adjusted instantly. It took several weeks for me to see how at peace she was in her new surroundings. I longed for the privacy of her room in The Manor.

The next afternoon I wheeled her on the sidewalk that led away from the hospital. We turned left at the T where sidewalk meets road. The sidewalk circled the hospital and wound around outside The Manor. Two nurses and Mr. Okabe, who lived in the room across the hall from Mom's old room, saw us walking by and waved wildly from an open window, "We miss you, Dorothy!" they hollered. I waved back and hollered, "We miss you, too!"

Mom lifted her hand in greeting then quietly said to me, "Keep moving, dearie."

"Oh, this whole business makes me so mad."

"Nancy, put the past behind you. Forget about The Manor."

After that day we turned right at the T and walked to Roosevelt Park overlooking downtown and islands in the Pacific Ocean. We watched fish boats flow through Metlakatla Pass on their way to and from fishing grounds. We watched tugs and freighters and ferries ply the harbour. We watched life carry on.

I tried to make her corner of the ward an expression of her life. Over the bed I hung the black and white photograph of her playing the organ. I hung the treble clef, a ceramic gift from two of her sons, above the photograph. I set an oval-framed photo of Dad on her dresser and I hung two photographs of her five children, one taken in 1948 and the other fifty years later. I hung a calendar with beautiful photographs of churches in Canada. The calendar was a gift from her friend, Helen. It brought satisfaction to me to bring some personality to her diminishing space on earth. But for Mom, none of it was necessary. "Please, no more, dearie. I don't want the clutter. I don't need anything. I'm happy just the way I am."

It surprised me to see how happy she was. She seemed to thrive on the constant activity around her. The regular routine of staff coming into the room, checking the women, teasing, talking, singing, touching, brought smiles to cheeks and laughter spilled from aged bodies. Mom asked for and received help in the morning to get her up and dressed. "I don't want to lie around in bed all day. I want to get up, get dressed and get my day started."

She willingly took part in activities. Singsongs, church services, birthday parties, luncheons, outings. I couldn't find her one late afternoon and was told that she had gone with others for Pub Night. She worked hard every day with Simon, the physiotherapist, struggling to walk back and forth on parallel bars.

When she wasn't busy with any of the numerous activities planned by staff or volunteers, she sat in her wheelchair beside her bed. It was covered with the quilt her granddaughter, Shirley, made for her when she moved into The Manor. Denise continued to bring Mom four books from the library every two weeks and she spent hours reading.

She befriended Sarah, the woman opposite her in the ward, who had suffered a stroke and had not regained her speech. Mom concerned herself when Sarah became unhappy and wheeled over and asked questions until Sarah smiled and nodded. Mom seemed to understand Sarah's grunts and sounds and conversed with her before returning to her own side of the room to continue reading her large-print books.

When I arrived late for Mom's ninety-first birthday party I was surprised to find her sitting beside her bed reading.

"Hi, Mom. Why aren't you at the party?" I asked.

"Hi, dearie. I was waiting for you."

"How come?"

"I want you to help me with Sarah. She doesn't want to go to the party and I don't want to leave her by herself. If you push her wheelchair we can all go to the party together."

"Good idea. Is that O.K. with you, Sarah?"

Sarah smiled and nodded.

Space was made for two more wheelchairs in the crowded living room. A chair was brought for me and squeezed in beside Mom. When the cake arrived with candles ablaze, everyone sang Happy Birthday, the words spilling easily off lips that in some cases could not remember names of family members anymore. Mom blew at the flaming candles again and again and finally said, "Help me, Sarah. Please help me blow out the candles." The two old women with heads together blew until all the candles were out. Cheers and clapping brought smiles and laughter. The cake was cut and juice was poured. Some of the residents were fed by family members, others by staff or volunteers. Icing was smeared across happy faces and licked from sticky fingers. Juice was spilled and crumbs littered the floor as we celebrated another milestone.

The woman who cut the residents' hair was also a pianist. She led the singsong of songs popular during the Depression and World War Two. The residents loved to sing the old songs. Although most of them couldn't remember anything current, the words from songs of their youth triggered memories and tears trickled down cheeks. There was applause before and after every song.

Although there were days of discomfort and unhappiness, especially after a death, most days were filled with kindness and goodness and a dignity for the old folk who were finishing life's cycle. Earthly possessions had no importance. A nurse rubbing cream into dry skin, or sweet smelling powder sprinkled and massaged tenderly onto humped shoulders, brought a comfort that no furnishings could provide.

It took weeks for me to achieve the grace that Mom had found easily after her move from The Manor. I don't know exactly when my transitions from anger to acceptance to agreement happened. But I know they were complete one day when I was leaving Mom's room and ran right into Mary. We were both surprised. Our immediate reaction was a firm and long hug.

"I won't say I'm sorry, Mary, because I'm not. But I will say you were right. It was time for Mom to move. She needed more help than I realized. This is a wonderful place. She is well looked after and she is truly happy here."

"You had me doubting myself, Nancy. I had a lot of sleepless nights. But I had to make the decision for your mom. She needed more help than she could get in intermediate care."

"Thank you, Mary. You were right."

The two chickens and the henhouse were gone when Mom awoke from the first of many "goofy" periods as I called them. They were harder on me than they were on her. She had such a good time but it broke my heart. She never appeared to have any recollection of the disturbances she created. If she did remember, she never said a word. She put it behind her.

I learned that death does follow dying. But not in any predictable fashion or any set time frame. Life is what happens while we are dying.

Mom was right. Life carries on.

Memories in a suitcase

I am ironing the blouses I wore on my summertime trip to New York with my son, Clinton. I am thinking about the choice of clothes I packed in my small suitcase – the suitcase I found beside a dumpster behind Clint's Vancouver apartment the day after we returned from our previous summer's trip to London and Paris.

"Hey, Clint, this looks like a perfectly good suitcase," I said as I leaned over to pick it up.

"Leave it, Mom. There's probably something the matter with it. No one would throw away a suitcase if it was any good."

I didn't want to leave it. I remembered my recent struggles through airports, and on and off trains with Mom's old suitcase. It has two small wheels on one end, so I thought I could pull it around with the attached strap instead of carrying it. But it kept falling over. This dumpster suitcase looks like the suitcases the airline attendants and pilots wheel behind them as they stride through airports. A compact, upright suitcase on sturdy wheels with a handle that extends and disappears with a flick of the wrist.

I didn't leave the suitcase behind. I threw it in the trunk of Clint's car. There is nothing the matter with it except the handle sticks about halfway and needs a good tug to get it all the way out. There is an extra zipper around the suitcase that extends the size.

One of my friends called me a dumpster diver later that day when I showed off my great find. "I didn't go IN the dumpster," I protested. "I found it ALONGSIDE the dumpster."

Clint wished afterwards that he'd found it. So I bought him a suitcase just like it for his thirty-fifth birthday. So we would both have a suitcase that we could take on the plane with us and avoid baggage delays on our flights to and from New York.

But there are drawbacks to a small suitcase. I could not pack anything extra. Not a change of shoes, an umbrella or raincoat. I laid out the clothes I wanted to take and then started the process of elimination.

I chose North Face pants that my friend Shannon found in the Salvation Army Thrift Shop for four dollars. Shannon is a world traveller and was a great help when I prepared for the London and Paris trip with Clint. I thought about her advice when I packed for New York. "Pack lightly. Don't take anything that needs ironing. Wear red. It looks great in photographs. Don't take that fleece jacket. It's too bulky."

The silk blouse I wore the first day in New York is one of the blouses I am ironing. I didn't listen to the ironing part of Shannon's advice but there is a lot of red in it. It's a crazy multicoloured blouse with odd shapes and patterns. I've had it for years. I've worn it to work, out for dinner, for family get-togethers. At times it gets forgotten in the closet and when I spot it, it's like meeting an old friend unexpectedly. I wonder why it's been so long since I've seen her. I have always enjoyed her company so much.

I wore the blouse on our flight to London last summer and this summer I wore it in New York when we took the subway to the Museum of Modern Art. I thought it was fitting to wear a bright, odd-looking blouse to a gallery that housed paintings by modern artists. My blouse was insignificant alongside huge canvases by Cy Twombly and Jackson Pollock. The feature exhibition was "Lee Bontecou, A Retrospective." I had never heard of Lee Bontecou's art, and now I'll never forget it. Her eccentric work is full of movement and imagination. I sensed the same freedom and abandonment when Clint and I visited the Picasso Museum in Paris the previous summer. How exciting to see paintings, sculpture, ceramics by one artist whose imagination and choice of media had no limits.

A burgundy blouse that I folded and placed in my suitcase was an unusual choice. I had only worn it once several years ago. I purchased black leather pants and a black leather jacket at a Boxing Day sale in Vancouver to wear on the motorcycle when Bill and I rode desert highways in the winter. Two young salesclerks brought different styles to the dressing room. Included with their choice of pants and jacket was a spandex burgundy blouse. Bill was kibitzing with the clerks when I came out of the dressing room. All three of them stopped talking when they saw me. I hadn't looked that young for a long time. I wanted the pants and jacket for motorcycle rides. I set the blouse aside. One of the young women said, "Today everything is half price and if you buy two items you get the third for free. You're taking that blouse."

I wore the burgundy blouse the second day in New York. The day we took the subway to the Guggenheim Museum and then walked to the Metropolitan Museum of Art. Clint told me later that day, when we sat together enjoying a beer in the Met Cafeteria, "Mom, I like your blouse, it looks good on you, and, what I really like, is that you are easy to spot in a crowd."

Shannon was right. It looks good in the photograph taken inside the Guggenheim standing beside a Brancusi sculpture. It looks good in the photograph of me sitting with a circle of black Rodin sculptures in the Met, in front of a Jackson Pollack painting, and between paintings by Picasso and Matisse.

We were tired at the end of that day. After our Happy Hour in the cafeteria we had returned to the gallery to view again the paintings of the Impressionists. We stayed until the lights were dimmed. We found our way to the main doors and walked down wide steps to Fifth Avenue, to the subway, Times Square, a deli, and home to a quiet hotel room where we stretched our legs out on our beds, with a cold beer in one hand and a deli wrap in the other.

I changed into my blue and white cotton caftan when we got back to the hotel. The same caftan I had packed so many times when Bill and I travelled to deserts in Baja and California. The same caftan I wore in Paris the night Clinton painted the small watercolour that now hangs in my kitchen.

We were in our air-conditioned hotel room in the middle of a heat wave, tired after a day of galleries and walking in the heat. We had taken the tube to Montmarte, walked up the well-photographed stairs to Sacre Couer and the art district. We walked narrow cobblestone streets. We spent hours at the Picasso Museum. We stopped for lunch at a sidewalk café and looked at old buildings covered with graffiti that looked artsy not angry. We walked to the Moulin Rouge. We walked until we couldn't walk anymore. We took the subway home to our lovely hotel and to our room facing a park where old men played chess and backgammon, young people played ping-pong and children played on swings. Where gendarmes blew their whistles at eight o'clock at night, everyone left the park and gates were locked. Where Clint sat on his bed with his legs stretched out and sketched while I sat at the dresser and painted. Clint joined me at the dresser and painted his sketching. I have his painting in front of the kitchen sink, where I see it every day. It reminds me of our time together in Europe. "For Mom From Paris ... Love, Clint."

Maybe that only happens once in a lifetime.

The white floral, cowboy-looking blouse I wore on the third day in New York didn't have a history when I packed it. I bought it on sale in Sears before we left. Now, as the iron erases wrinkles, I think of it as my New York blouse. It got initiated in the crowded streets, subways and galleries of New York City. When Clint opened the drapes of our hotel room that Saturday morning, he exclaimed, "Mom, come here. You've got to see this." Seventh Avenue was alive with a mass of people who swarmed through a gigantic flea market that filled both sides of the street for blocks.

We joined the crowd and jostled our way to our favourite breakfast deli for freshly squeezed orange juice. We fought our way through the crowd to get to the subway that took us to the Upper East Side and the Whitney Museum of American Art. We looked at paintings so realistic they could have been photographs. We looked at paintings that were so beautiful or haunting it was hard to pull our eyes from them. We looked at abstract art that mystified but entranced the eye.

We rested our tired legs and feet in the gallery cafe. Like our time together in the pubs of London the previous summer, we sat and talked about our lives and our feelings. Sometimes a distance from home brings home into sharp focus. I talked about Mom, our relationship and her relationship with her siblings.

I told Clint about Mom's joy when her brother, Bob, visited her when she was in her early nineties and Bob was in his late eighties. As she wheeled her chair towards him, tears streamed down her face. Tears welled up in Bob's eyes as he watched her approach. They hugged and held hands and talked all afternoon. Bob brought photographs of their childhood home in Calgary. They were recent photos and Mom and Bob could barely see the house because of a huge tree in the front yard. They laughed when they reminisced about the tree. Their father planted it as a sapling when their sister, Joyce, won a spelling bee as a young child. I told Clint I want the same for myself; a warm, joyful relationship with my siblings who share memories of a childhood no one experienced the way we did, who knew how much "home plate" in our front yard annoyed Mom. Despite her best efforts and constant complaints, grass never grew there.

I mentioned Bill and his two brothers, Roy and Robert, and how, when they get together, they laugh about the same stories again and again. No one gets the same delight as they do, although the story about Roy trying to drown Robert in the bathtub by sitting on his head always makes me laugh. Their dad got fed up listening to the squabbling, stormed into the bathroom and swatted the first thing he saw which was the drowning Robert's rear end.

I told Clint I want good relationships with my brothers as senior years unfold. Siblings with whom to share memories of childhood as we grow old. I told Clint how my relationship with Mom affected me and how it affected my hopes for the future.

Suddenly we realized the future was now and our rested feet walked us back to the Met. We needed a second chance to see the Impressionist and Modern paintings in this wonderful museum of art. We needed to stamp the blaze of colour and abstract design of the huge canvases of Gorky, de Kooning, Pollock and Mitchell firmly in our memory.

When we reached our saturation point, we walked out of the Met into sunshine. We had forgotten another world existed. Our weary feet led us through Central Park, a part of New York fringed by skyscrapers but a natural world complete in itself. We ended up at Jake's Dilemma, a pub on the Upper West Side, five minutes before Happy Hour. It was Clint's round but I suggested that he wait a few minutes so he would get half price beer. "I'm not sitting here without a beer," he said, "and it's so close to five o'clock, I'm sure I'll get the Happy Hour price." Those two mugs of beer cost him nine dollars. When it was my round, it cost me four-fifty. We laughed and remembered our first evening in Paris. How it was his round and he got stuck with the bill for our first and only beer at a sidewalk café in the tourist district of Les Halles after my introduction to the Pompidou, the National Museum of Modern Art, and after walking across bridges over the Seine and along cobblestone streets bordered with old buildings and fountains and spiraled churches. Those two beer cost him fifteen Euros, about twenty-five dollars. We didn't make that mistake again. On our walk back to the hotel we stopped at a Mono Prix and bought a half dozen beer to keep in the small fridge in our room.

Shannon would be pleased to know I did pack one blouse that didn't need ironing although there's not a hint of red in it. It's a dressy looking blouse. I bought it one spring before starting my seasonal job in the office of the shipyard in town. It is a comfortable office with big windows overlooking boats hauled up out of the water and boats tied up at docks in the harbour. I sat at an antique wooden desk and typed invoices on a typewriter. While I typed I listened to the tap, tap, tap of Bob or Gary caulking wooden boats. A steady rhythm like the harmonious flow of the shipyard. Boats hauled up and down with the motion of the tide. Up for a shave and a haircut, the term for a boat to be pressure washed and copper painted. The cadence of the words I typed over and over: starboard side, sister frame, bow stem, underbody of the hull. Boats alive with names like Lionheart and Sandpiper, and parts called ratline, spider legs, bat wing, pigtail, beavertail, steering ram, locking dog, wildcat, butterfly valve.

Wooden stairs and hand railings inside the shipyard were grooved and worn smooth after four generations of shipwrights' weathered hands and work boots climbed up and down on their daily tasks. Shavings from power saws curled under tables like dust under a bed.

When I started working at the shipyard there were girlie posters wallpapering the crew's coffee room. As the years passed the posters slowly disappeared and bumper stickers replaced centerfolds. "Eat Moose. 12,000 Wolves Can't Be Wrong."

After work I drove to The Manor to visit Mom. When I arrived wearing this blouse, she said, "My, don't you look nice. I love that blouse." When I wore it a few years later, after she was moved to extended care, she asked, "Did you get a new blouse? It's lovely."

It was a sunny Sunday morning when I wore the blouse in New York. We boarded the subway and rode to the southern end of Manhattan. It was an eerie feeling to be underground in a subway car that made no stops for a section of the route. We were advised several times that we could get out at a certain station north of where the World Towers had dominated the New York skyline, but there would be no stops until Bowling Green, the station south of the catastrophe. The beauty of the day stunned us as we climbed up the stairs from the underground. We walked to Ground Zero. It was the silence that startled me. People peered through wire mesh fencing that surrounded the area and talked in whispers. It was impossible not to recall the vivid images of planes crashing into the towers and the towers crumbling down.

Clint and I had seen submissions of architectural models to replace the towers in the Royal Academy of Arts Gallery in London. Imaginative and impressive designs displayed as part of the "Summer Exhibition", an exhibition of contemporary art that absorbed us for hours. We saw the chosen model at the Museum of Modern Art in its temporary location in Queen's on our first day in New York.

As I stood at Ground Zero, all I could see was a huge area of bare ground circled by skyscrapers, many with scaffolding and idle cranes alongside used to repair damage caused by 9/11. There was no repair or construction happening this beautiful Sunday morning. My mind was stuck on the tragedy and could not envision, as completed structures, any of the models we had seen.

We walked miles again that day. We walked through the financial district with its many modern sculptures. Clint took my photograph beside a North Coast totem pole (carved by Gitxsan artists Walter Harris and Art Sterritt) standing in the One Chase Manhattan Plaza. I took his photograph beside a massive sculpture by Jean Dubuffet and again in front of a sculpture by Roy Lichtenstein. We walked through Chinatown, Little Italy, Soho, Greenwich Village, Chelsea and soaked up the architecture and ethnicity along the narrow streets and winding alleys. In Soho, street artists displayed their art and we sauntered along both sides of the street for blocks looking at the various exhibits. We stopped at Washington Square to listen to a jam session by several musicians of varying ages. We walked till we reached the Flatiron Building in Chelsea. I wanted to see the world's first true skyscraper. We were tourists in a city that catered to tourists. We went on a harbour cruise to see the skyline from the water and to see the Statue of Liberty. We went to the top of the Empire State Building to see the view in daylight and the lights at night. Every day brimmed over.

The last day in New York we decided to visit private galleries. I took my last clean blouse off its hanger. It is a well-travelled blouse. I bought it in Hawaii the winter Bill and I spent three months there. It was the year of the first Gulf War and military presence on Oahu was evident everywhere. Old war movies played endlessly on television.

I walked often to the Honolulu Art Gallery, enthralled to see original works of art by Impressionists, rooms full of antique furniture, a separate section of Modern art and a comprehensive collection of Chinese art. I walked to see art in shops and in private galleries. I walked to see all the hula shows. I walked to see architecture and walked to see flowers and gardens and fountains surrounded by tropical growth.

Bill and I swam every day, sometimes twice a day. Mid-afternoon we took our flippers to the beach and swam out to the surfers. At first the surf scared me. I fought it and swallowed mouthfuls of salt water. Then one day I saw a turtle in the surf, leisurely waving his legs back and forth. It was a magnificent moment. I relaxed after that and swam with joy instead of fear. I've thought of that turtle many times since. Whenever I swim in salt water where surf rolls onto shore or whenever I get a cramp in my foot when swimming laps in a pool, I close my eyes, see the turtle in the surf off Waikiki Beach and relax.

Sometimes Bill and I took the bus to Ala Moana Beach, put on our flippers and swam for a mile along the shore and back again. We wore long-sleeved cotton shirts over our bathing suits to protect our skin from the sun. We changed into dry clothes when we got back, lay on the hot sand and let the sun warm our cold bodies. When the chill left us, we walked across the highway to the Makai Market on the bottom floor of the Ala Moana Shopping Centre. Food from every country rimmed the huge area and in the middle were chairs and long tables. We chose our meal then searched for two empty chairs.

After lunch we went back to the park across the street and napped on the grass under the shade of a banyan tree. We dozed to the sounds of birds and traffic and children playing and palms swaying. Later we walked home along the waterfront. Bill liked to wander along the docks to see sailboats moored at the Yacht Club and he timed it perfectly to arrive at a pub close by for a pitcher of half price beer at Happy Hour.

One day as we walked past a small shop I spotted a white, long sleeved, Chinese style blouse with big, pink and blue flowers splashed all over it. I couldn't resist. The blouse was a constant companion the winters we camped on beaches in Baja. We swam almost every day there, too. Bill checked the sailboats with his binoculars and if he spotted a sailboat flying a Canadian flag we put on our wetsuits and flippers and swam out to say hello. Bill had to give me a shove on my behind as I pulled myself up the rope ladder thrown over the side in greeting. We had wonderful visits with new friends from Canada sitting on decks of luxurious sailboats anchored in beautiful bays, soaking in the warmth of the sun and smelling salt sea breeze. I always felt a tinge of loneliness after we swam back and watched the sailboat slowly fade away.

We swam often to rocky areas. Along with our wetsuits and flippers, we had our masks and snorkels. The natural splendour of tropical fish never ceased to fascinate us. On my fiftieth birthday in January of 1994, Bill asked, "What do you want to do on your birthday?" I answered, "I want to go snorkeling." Ken, another camper, wanted to come with us. He wasn't a strong swimmer and we had to swim slower than we normally would have. I was impatient and wanted to swim ahead. Bill said, "No, we have to stay together in the ocean." At the rocks the snorkeling was as delightful as ever but when we started our swim back, I got impatient again. I swam ahead and Bill called me back. For him it must have been a bit like fishing, trying to reel me in. Finally he said, "O.K. go ahead but stay close to shore." Impatience left my body with the ease and freedom of the swim back. The wind had blown up while we were gone and surf crashed on shore. I thought if I took my flippers off I might be able to ride the surf up onto the beach and avoid getting my flippers covered in sand. It might have worked except when I put my bare foot down I startled a stingray. When its tail hit my inside arch I thought I'd stepped on a broken bottle. Venom released into my body paralyzed me. I couldn't stumble through the surf and get to shore. Bill and Ken arrived, dragged me out of the water and up the beach. I will never forget the shock and excruciating pain suffered as a result of my impatience.

After days full of hiking and swimming I put on the long-sleeved, cotton blouse I bought in Hawaii with a pair of white cotton, drawstring pants I bought at a market in Ensenada. Sometimes I'd walk the beach to search for perfect shells. Sometimes I'd walk to photograph shadowed rocks in the late afternoon sunshine. Sometimes Bill and I walked to visit other campers or we walked to a small, palm frond cantina and ordered, "Dos cervezas, por favor." We relaxed in the shade, listened to the breeze rustle palm fronds and watched as the sunset turned the sky to pink and blue pastels.

After fifteen years of wearing this blouse on beaches in Baja, and hiking and exploring trails in southern California and Arizona, it covered my arms in a heat wave in London when Clint and I walked to see the Parliament Buildings and Westminster Abbey. We walked past 10 Downing Street on our way to the National Art Gallery where there was a constant crowd in front of Van Gogh's *Sunflowers* and A *Wheatfield with Cypresses*. Rembrandt's self portraits dominated a room full of his rich paintings. In another room I was attracted to Ruben's muted and swirling canvases and didn't realize until my nose was up close that the swirls were angels.

After walking and standing all morning, we left the gallery and looked for an air-conditioned pub. London is the place to find good pubs and The Salisbury turned out to be the nicest pub we found in London. The warmth of wood mingled with stained glass, comfortable booths and art on the walls. We sat together drinking our beer and discussed the art we'd seen at the National Gallery that morning and at the Tate Modern and the Courtauld the day before. I told Clint how fortunate I was to have a son who would take his mom on a trip to London and Paris to visit art galleries. A son who studied and taught art history. A son who waited patiently for me when I got lost in the Musée d'Orsay after descending a spiral staircase to use the washroom. I got twisted around and climbed back up a different spiral staircase and ended up on a higher level. I could see Clint sitting with his arms and legs crossed when I peered over the balcony but I had no idea which staircase in that beautiful museum to take in order to reach him. A son who was my personal tour guide as well as my companion.

We had tears that day sitting in the Salisbury Pub out of the sweltering mid-day heat. We had tears for Katherine, Clint's Katherine, who had suffered a massive stroke a month before our planned trip to Europe. Clint had tears as he faced the thought of losing her. I had tears when I saw my son's distress. The tears flowed easily, constantly, as we discussed Katherine while she lay in a bed at G.F. Strong Rehabilitation Centre in Vancouver. We tried to reason our way out of the guilt we felt for still going through with our plans. She wanted us to. If we had cancelled our long talked about trip she would have felt the guilt we were experiencing. We knew she would need Clint more when she recovered enough to return home. She was in good hands, but all the reasons in the world could not erase the guilt we felt for not cancelling our trip.

A year later, after intensive therapy helped Katherine to talk and walk again, Clint and I travelled to New York City. I wore the same pink and blue blouse I had worn a year earlier in London. Despite our casual appearance, we were treated like millionaires when we visited private galleries that day in New York. Galleries that exhibited the best of modern artists – Frank Stella, Lee Krasner, Mark Rothko, Lee Bontecou. A Joan Miro mural hung in the foyer of a skyscraper where we had to pass security before getting in an elevator to reach a private gallery. The security wasn't as stringent as the day we went to the Jewish Museum to see a major exhibition by Modigliani. There we were wanded like people going through airport security.

I had made arrangements to meet Stephanie, the daughter of my girlfriend, Joy, after visiting the private galleries on our last day in New York. Joy and I went to school together when we were growing up in Nelson. As teenagers, we spent hours together. If I was at her house, she walked me halfway home, and if she was at my house, I walked her halfway home. Halfway was Hume School. Sometimes she was allowed to stay for supper before I walked her to the school. She was a bit intimidated by my four older brothers and they loved to tease her, "After we make merry, we'll all jump for joy."

Joy and I have stayed friends the forty-five years since we graduated from high school. Although we rarely see one another, we write letters that keep our friendship intact. I had not seen Stephanie since she was a child but when I saw her standing outside the Heartland Brewery, I was overcome with emotion. It could have been Joy standing there many years ago when I had last seen her.

We spent a delightful two hours together. Clint and Stephanie, both in their mid-thirties, both full of life and opinions, talked nonstop. I watched and listened but seeing Stephanie had taken me back to my childhood, and when I talked it was mostly about Joy and about our youth together.

Stephanie had an appointment so she walked us back to our hotel and hailed a cab. We hugged before she stepped into a yellow taxi. She disappeared into the busy street, into a sea of yellow taxis. She disappeared like the sailboats into the horizon and I had that same twinge of loneliness.

On our flight home, after we made the dash to our connecting flight in Toronto, Clint said, "You are a terrific travelling companion, Mom."

I replied, "You are, too, Clint."

The blouses now rest on their hangers. I wonder where they will take me next.

communications addressed to the Superintendent
ome Tax must have sufficient postage affixed.

Form No. 1
105M/12-36.
or use of individuals

PROVINCE OF ALBERTA
INCOME TAX

1936

RECEIVED

r use of Department

Occupational Code No. ....
Income Code No. ....
For use of Department

Return is to be prepared in duplicate. One copy is to be retained by the taxpayer and one copy must be delivered or mailed, postpaid
the Superintendent of Income Tax, QU'APPELLE BUILDING, EDMONTON, ALTA., on or before 31st MARCH, 1937.

PRINT NAME AND ADDRESS PLAINLY BELOW

(Surname) (Christian)

dress of present residence

(Street and Number) (City or Town)

is essential that taxpayers notify the Superintendent of Income Tax of any subsequent change in address.
filing this return such new address should be given.)

on or nature of business of Taxpayer

ed state name and address of employer during 1936
of business or professional practice during 1936 state:

Business name

ames of partners (if any) Business address

Was an audit made of your books for the year 1936?   (Yes or no)

esidence during 1935

ther married or unmarried, widow or widower   If status was changed during 1936, give date

during 1936; give date   Maiden name of wife   Income of wife after marriage $

ages of children, under the age of 21 years as at December 31st, 1936, dependent on you for support:

NAME	AGE	Income (if any)	NAME	AGE	Income (if any)

ependents (i.e. parent, grandparent, son, daughter, brother or sister) over 21 years of age mentally or physically incapacitated.
Form No. 20 for each dependent claimed

wife
usband) in full

Vife $ Income of Husband   (wife/husband) was dependent upon you in 1936

ster any property or securities to your (wife/husband) or children during 1936?   If so, give particulars.

Construction

zone

Superintendent of Income Tax only						Per Ret. of Taxpayer	For Use of Dept.
tal	Tax	Pen.	Int.	Intis		$	$
					Gross Income (See Item No. 12)		
					Deductions (See Item No. 20)		
					Net Income		
					Less Statutory exemption (See below) $		
					Allowance for dependent children under 21 years of age at $400 each $		

Pen.	Int.		Totals
		Due	
		Paid	
		Bal.	
Initials			
Date	Approved by		

Allowance for amount contributed for the support of dependents over 21 years of age, mentally or physically infirm (maximum $400 for each dependent) $

Income subject to tax

Tax Payable (See Schedule of Rates, Page 4)

Allowance for Income Tax paid other Provinces

Penalty for Incomplete Returns

Penalty for Late Filing

Total Amount to be Paid

tify that this, my income tax return for the year 1936, is a full and complete disclosure of my total income from all sources,
tion given herein, together with supplementary statements and additional schedules and documents attached, if any, are
ect and that the expenditures claimed were actually incurred.

193 Telephone Number   Business
                        Residence

Signature

Remittance enclosed herewith $

a) For failure to file return by 31st MARCH, 1937, 5% of the tax payable. Maximum penalty $500.
) For incomplete compilation of this or any supplemental form, 1% of the tax payable. Minimum $1.00, maximum $20.00.

STATUTORY EXEMPTIONS
1,500—Where a husband and wife each have a separate income of $750, separate returns must be
or husband or wife has an income of less
750—A return and such claim, an exemption of $750.
750—A claim by an unmarried person, widow or widower, for the maximum exemption of $1,500 can on
the taxpayer has dependent upon him and resident

*O*n my early morning walk, I ignore "No Trespassing" and "No Loitering" signs alongside the construction of a new canal. The construction is a certainty. I watch as huge machines dig deep into the earth to create a new route for water to flow. The details of the construction are rumour. It is rumoured that thirty-two miles of new canal will be constructed at a cost of thirty-five million dollars. It is also rumoured the new canal will be concrete as eight million dollars worth of water is leaking daily, or yearly, depending on who is doing the telling, in the old, dirt-bottomed canal.

I am fascinated with the construction. I watch each new step. Only once has it been brought to my attention that I am trespassing. "Can't you read?" asks a voice from under a yellow hardhat. I leave but return the next morning to watch a giant long-necked crane lift and place rebar into the huge trench dug deep into the earth. I think of Mom on my early morning walks. The construction of a new canal would interest her and, in earlier years, she would have documented each step.

Throughout my thirties and half of my forties, Mom and Dad went for afternoon drives regularly. They drove around town and they drove Highway 16 along the Skeena River. Mom carried their small plastic camera in her purse. When they saw any construction, she photographed the scene and the heavy equipment. Her photographs were not artistic. They were a record of what was being built or changed, whether the construction of a new hotel or the widening of a highway. She showed the photographs when family visited and described the projects in detail.

I wasn't interested in her construction photographs. Nor was I interested in the description of the construction. I endured the slide shows that flashed from the projector onto the collapsible screen. The entertainment was the rough treatment Mom and Dad gave their equipment as they bashed the side of the projector if a slide got stuck, or when they bickered if they couldn't get the screen set up properly.

"Oh, Ole, not like that," Mom complained.

"Don't tell me how to do it. You don't know everything."

"Watch what you're doing!" Mom screeched as the screen tumbled over and knocked the lamp off their television.

Once they ironed out their problems they sat holding hands while bulldozers with huge tires pushed gigantic rocks into the Skeena River or cranes lifted steel girders high into place for a new shopping centre. Dad controlled the wired remote that clicked one slide after another onto the screen. Peace lasted as long as this part of the operation ran smoothly. If he went too fast, Mom demanded, "Slow down, Ole. I can't finish the description when you go that fast." If he didn't go fast enough, she insisted, "Hurry up, Ole. We'll be here all night at this pace." When a slide stuck in the projector, she moaned, "Oh, Ole. Now what."

His fingers pushed the reverse and forward buttons on the remote in his attempt to dislodge the slide. If that didn't work, he banged the remote on the table on which the projector was balanced. If that failed, his hand bashed the side of the projector until the slide fell into place. For a stubborn slide, Mom added to the punishment. Her hand hammered the projector from her side while Dad swung at it on his side. Eventually the slide show resumed and Mom's commentary continued as if nothing had happened.

The canal road has been widened. It is a mess of ruts and mounds. Sprinkling systems, stretched on top of huge mounds of dirt, spray water twenty-four hours a day. Watering trucks bounce along the rough road and water sprays out in their wake. When we first arrive in southern California Bill asks a man driving a truck with California license plates why water is pumped out of the canal and sprinkled day and night on mounds of dirt piled high alongside the canal road.

"It's to keep the dust down," he drawls. "It's a law in California. You have to keep the dust down."

The March Dad turned seventy-five, he said, "That's it. I don't have to do anything anymore."

Mom asked, "What do you mean you don't have to do anything anymore?"

"Just that. I don't have to do anything I don't want to do anymore. I don't have to do my income tax. They can throw me in jail for all I care. I'm not doing it."

"You have to do your income tax," Mom argued.

"No, I don't. I don't have to pay bills anymore, either."

"Yes, you do. You can't ignore bills."

"Yes, I can. They can throw me in jail. I'm not doing it anymore. I've had it."

"But Ole, what about the hydro bill and the utilities? They have to be paid."

"You can pay them if you want, but I'm not, and no one's going to make me."

When Mom phoned and repeated this conversation to me I had to hold the phone away from my ear. "I don't understand what's the matter with him. He knows I don't know how to do income tax or pay bills. That's always been his job."

"He'll be all right, Mom. He probably doesn't feel like tackling paperwork today. Give him a couple of days and he'll be fine."

—

Gumbo sticks to the bottom and sides of my running shoes. With every step more gumbo accumulates and my leg muscles strain to pick up the extra weight. I shouldn't have come along the freshly watered canal road this morning. I struggle towards the construction site, curious to see what work has been completed in the last twenty-four hours.

Framing with the rebar has started. I think work should progress at a faster rate. It will take forever at this pace. I take a photograph before leaving. I pull my feet, step by step, out of gumbo until I reach the embankment that separates the canal road from the gravel county road. I shuffle my feet along the gravel to dislodge the thick, sticky mud from my shoes. I stop at a big rock and rub the sides of my shoes against the firm surface. I cannot get all the gumbo off my shoes.

—

Mom phoned again two days later. "There's something the matter with Dad. He's not himself. All he wants to do is sit in front of that darned television."

"I'll come after work. Maybe he's not feeling well."

"He looks fine to me. It's his job to get the income tax done. I've given him all my music books and receipts and he's ignoring them. He can't ignore them if I want to keep on teaching music."

"I'll come after work. Don't worry about the income tax. I'll do it for you if he won't."

"But what about the bills? He's ignoring them, too."

"I'll talk to him. If he won't do it, I'll show you how to pay them. There's nothing to it."

"That's not the point. It's his job. He can't just sit there and watch television the rest of his life."

When I arrived after work, Mom was teaching in her music room. Dad was watching television. He wore his good sports jacket and a shirt and tie. His face was clean-shaven. His intertwined fingers rested on his dress pants. He smiled when he saw me. "Hi, honey. All done for the day?"

"Hi, Dad," I said as I leaned over to kiss him. "I'm all done the working-for-a-living part anyway."

"That's good."

"How are things going with you?"

"Fine, honey."

"Good." I settled myself on the couch. "Think I'll look at my income tax this weekend. Have you started yours yet?"

"No. I'm not going to start it."

"How come?"

"I'm not doing it anymore."

"Oh. You want some help?"

"No. I don't need help. I'm not doing it anymore. They can throw me in jail for all I care. I'm not doing it."

"You don't have to, Dad. I'll do it for you."

"Suit yourself."

—

I don't walk the canal road to check the construction site for two days. I walk in the wash where deep, course sand gradually erases gumbo from my shoes. My footsteps disturb long-eared jackrabbits that spring from underbrush and, in giant leaps, bound over the dunes. Startled lizards freeze against speckled rocks. Birds flit from leafless branches on twisted trees. The rising sun briefly turns earth to gold and on the dunes desert flowers cast long shadows on rippled sand. Music fills the air as what sounds like a million birds pronounce the glory of the day.

By the time my shoes are clean two days later, I am walking the canal road that has dried in the sun-filled desert climate. I cannot understand my need to see the construction site.

—

I phoned Mom in the evening. Dad answered the phone that sat on a table between his La-Z-Boy chair and Mom's chair. I could barely hear his voice over the noise of the television.

"Hi, Dad. Is Mom there?"

"She's down in the basement. Just a minute."

I took the phone from my ear knowing he would holler at the top of his lungs, "Mom! Mom!"

When Mom picked up the extension phone downstairs, Dad dropped the phone back it its cradle. "I wish he wouldn't do that," she complained, "and I wish he wouldn't yell at me like that, either."

The extra phone in the basement allowed Mom to talk about Dad without him hearing. It had been installed when she got older so she wouldn't have to run up and down stairs to answer the phone if she was doing laundry or sewing.

"I talked to Dad while you were teaching."

"Yes, he told me you were here."

"I told him I would look after the income tax for him."

"I wish you wouldn't do that. It's his job. He doesn't do anything anymore. He just sits in front of that blaring television all day."

"Well, he wasn't unpleasant with me but he certainly was adamant. It sounds like he isn't going to do it. I can leave it for another week or two and see if he changes his mind but I can't leave it too long."

"I know, dearie. I appreciate your offer. I'll see if I can get him interested in the next few days. He hasn't paid any bills yet, either, so I'll have to get after him about that too."

"I didn't mention the bills. I figure something's upset him and he'll get back to the paper work when he gets over it."

"What if he doesn't?"

"Then we'll deal with it."

Clouds move across desert sky and change the colouring of mountains to shades of purple and blue. During the night rain pelts the roof of our trailer. Gumbo will now keep me from walking the canal road. It will be another two or three days before I can return to see what progress has taken place at the construction site.

Despite Mom's harping, Dad never completed another income tax return or paid another bill. I told Mom I would wait until the last Saturday in April and if Dad had not changed his mind, I would look after their finances.

When I arrived at Mom and Dad's home, Mom was ready for me. All her papers concerned with teaching piano and theory were piled on the kitchen table. While Dad sat watching television in the living room, Mom and I sat knee to knee while I organized their income tax return. It was the first time in my life that Mom did not scold me about how I was doing something or suggest how I could be doing it differently. I completed the profit and loss statement for her teaching and filled in the blanks on their joint income tax return. When I was finished I took it to Dad to sign.

"I don't want anything to do with it," he said.

"You have to sign it, Ole," Mom argued.

"No, I don't," he replied.

I took the papers back into the kitchen and asked Mom to sign it.

"Why me?" she asked. "It's his job."

"It's in your name, too," I said. "It will be fine if you sign it."

"Where do I sign?"

"Right here," I pointed to the line at the bottom of the return.

"Do I sign Dorothy M or Dorothy May?"

"Whatever you like."

"I use Dorothy May on my music business," she said, "so I'll use Dorothy M for the financial business." At seventy-two years of age, she wrote Dorothy M. Borch on an income tax return for the first time in her life.

"I want to pay you for this," she said as she handed me the finished paperwork.

"You don't have to pay me," I said as I gathered forms and put them inside the envelope supplied in the tax package.

"I know I don't have to. I want to. Where's Dad's chequebook?"

———

I fasten the straps on my Tilley hat under my chin and at the back of my neck. Wind gusts along the canal and I do not want to lose my hat into the pit in the ground with its newly poured cement. It is Saturday morning and the construction site is quiet. I walk the ridge of the pit and photograph shadows cast by rebar on cement. I walk back to the road and look at bundles of rebar lying on the ground. Wire is twisted around the bundles, and strips of paint colour a small portion of the rebar. The variety of colours makes me think this is a code to help with the placement of each bundle into the hole in the ground, like the coloured ends on the branches of an artificial Christmas tree. I photograph lines created by rebar, wire and paint. I walk to the side of the road where large piles of rusted, twisted metal have been heaped and photograph designs in the rust that look like Jackson Pollock paintings. A smoke tree struggles under carelessly dropped, rusted metal. The tree's spine is crushed and broken but its wispy branches reach into the air.

—

Dad's filing system for bills was meticulous. His records were perfect. His pens and pencils, rulers and letter opener lay tidily beside his covered adding machine on a shelf beside his filing cabinet in the back porch off their kitchen. Only the current month's bills lay scattered on the secretary in the living room.

"Do you want to open these bills, Dad?" I asked as I sorted through the mail.

"No thanks, honey," he answered as if I'd asked him if he'd wanted a cup of tea.

"I guess I'll show Mom how to pay them if you don't mind."

"I don't mind, honeybunch. You do what you like. You can leave them right there as far as I'm concerned. It won't bother me."

"I don't want to upset you, Dad. I don't want to interfere. You've always looked after the finances."

His eyes left the television and he smiled at me. "You're not upsetting me. I'm happy you're helping Mom. She's the one who's upset. She hasn't stopped nagging me for weeks. I'm getting sick of it. I wish she'd do it, or forget it, and shut up about it. I'm not doing it anymore and that's that. I don't care if she doesn't do it, either. They aren't going to throw us both in jail."

"I think I'll help Mom so that I don't have to visit you in jail," I teased. "Where do you keep your chequebook?"

He smiled again. "It's in the filing cabinet with the bank statements."

I gathered the bills and took them into the kitchen where Mom sat waiting. His eyes returned to the flickering television screen.

"What took you so long? Did you get the chequebook?"

"I was just making sure Dad didn't mind me interfering."

"It's too bad if he minds. He's the one who started all this trouble."

I ignored the comment and went to the back porch to open the filing cabinet. The chequebook was on top of a bundle of bank statements wrapped together with an elastic band on each end. Paid bills were filed alphabetically with the cheque number and date of payment written on them with Dad's distinctive handwriting. I brought the chequebook, the letter opener and his pen into the kitchen and settled myself next to Mom.

"I'll use my own pen," she said and got up and went into her music room. She returned with her pen and letter opener. "You can put his stuff back."

"Later," I said. "Let's get to work."

We sat side by side while Mom received her first lesson in bookkeeping with the television blaring in the background.

Black clouds gather and chase across desert sky. Thunder rumbles and wind blows hard and long. No awnings are out on the variety of motorhomes and trailers scattered across the desert. Unattended tarpaulins, whipped by the wind, flap noisily all day. Lawn chairs clatter over desert sand and collect at the base of trees and bushes. Small birds chatter on swaying branches while large birds hang stationary in the sky. Their wings waver in the wind. By evening lightening flashes over distant mountains. The storm circles until the flash of lightening and the crack of thunder become one. I go to bed with the noise of wind rattling and shaking the trailer. Sleep comes with the steady sound of unrelenting wind. Rain pounds on the roof and jolts me awake during the night. This is not gentle rain that settles dust. This is rain that squashes and breaks flowers and creates flash floods that wipe out highways and homes. It rains hard all night and all the next day. Twice during the day I attempt to go for a walk but any letup is brief and I'm chased home through rivers of water moving wildly across the ground while rain pelts down on me.

The rain stops sometime during the second night. I wake to light around the edges of blinds and to silence. I want to walk to see the construction site despite the gumbo I know will be thick and deep. I put on my running shoes and head out into sunshine through puddles and moving water. When I reach the canal road, my legs struggle against the magnetic pull of the sticky mud. By the time I arrive at the construction site, my shoes are caked. I stare in disbelief. What was once a huge cavity in the earth is now a lake. There is no sign of construction. No rebar, no cement, no equipment. Only a few wooden planks float on foamy water.

—

Mom added her new job of looking after the finances to the list of necessary chores that had to be done. Like dishes had to be washed and beds made before leaving the house, bills had to be paid when they arrived in the mail. She was messier than Dad. Her piles weren't exact or her pens and pencils straight. But she caught on quickly to the idea of money coming in and going out. She recorded cheques written and received. The bank reconciliation was done monthly after the bank statement arrived in the mail.

Dad had given Mom a monthly cash allowance for fifty years. With that money she bought food and clothing and all the household necessities. Dad looked after the purchase of houses, cars, furniture, maintenance and insurance. They discussed major items and holidays, but it was Dad who made final decisions. If Mom got too demanding, Dad reminded her, "You're not running my life."

But after Dad refused to look after the finances, it appeared that Mom was running his life. She had been given total control over all aspects. Dad's only insistence was his lottery ticket twice a week. Mom walked to the corner store begrudgingly every Wednesday and Saturday with ten dollars for his Lotto 649 ticket. "This is a waste of money, Ole. I don't see why we need to spend so much money on lottery tickets."

She spent money differently than Dad. She gave more money to the church, to charities, to public television. When I prepared their income tax return annually, I commented that some of their expenses were not bills but requests for money.

"You have to read the fine print, Mom. You don't have to pay every piece of paper that comes through the mail slot."

"We're doing fine, thanks, dearie. We have enough money."

"That's not the point. You could end up with a major expense if your furnace stops working or your roof starts leaking. You should put some money aside."

"I'll be more careful."

—

I do not return to the construction site. There is only silence along the canal. I walk down the wash and photograph patterns left in sand by rushing, swirling water. On the dunes, I look for shadows to photograph but coyotes have hunted along the dunes and their tracks spoil new ripples formed by the storm.

Wind rattling Venetian blinds on our open trailer windows wakes me at dawn. I hope it has blown hard enough during the night for fine sand to cover coyote tracks. The rising sun is already hot as I scurry over moguls and through trees and bush. Deep sand slows my steps when I reach the wash. By the time I arrive at the dunes my breathing is heavier and my t-shirt is damp with perspiration. A sudden breeze cools my body. My heart beats faster as I climb the soft, fine sand of the dunes. Yesterday's tracks are gone. I see ripples and curves accentuated by the early morning angle of the sun as I look up to the rounded ridge at the top of the dunes. Almost at the top I stop as I see small tracks, like miniature bicycle tires, winding every which way over the exquisitely formed ripples. Birds hunting small insects have spoiled the new formations. I leave the dunes without taking a photograph. It is impossible to be angry at birds singing from tops of twisted trees, their heads lifted, mouths open, as they fill the wash with music.

—

Mom phoned me at work in the afternoon.

"I don't like to bother you when you're working but I thought you'd want to know that Dad fell this morning."

"Did he hurt himself?"

"He hit his head on the kitchen counter when he fell. There was blood everywhere."

"Oh, Mom. You should have phoned earlier."

"I called an ambulance. They stitched him up in emergency and bandaged his head."

"Is he in the hospital?"

"Oh, no. I called a cab and brought him home. I can look after him. I wanted you to know in case you heard there was an ambulance here. I don't want you to worry."

"Is there anything I can do?"

"Not right now. But Dad says he wants to see you after work."

"I'll be there."

I wasn't prepared to see Dad looking so good. He was sitting in his chair watching television and, aside from the bandage circling his head, he looked the same as any other day. I could hear the halting sound of a child's hands on piano keys so I knew Mom was teaching.

"Hi, Dad," I said as I entered the living room.

"Hi, honey. How are you today?"

"I'm fine. How are you?"

"I'm fine now I guess. I wasn't so good this morning."

"That's what I hear. What happened?"

"I don't know. I blanked out. Didn't even feel it coming. But I know one thing. It's time to get my papers in order. After work on Friday I want you to take Mom and me to the bank. I want you and Mom to have signing authority on all my accounts and my safety deposit box. I want everything organized so that if something happens to me, there won't be any trouble for Mom. Would you do that for me?"

"Of course, Dad."

"I know Mom's all right now with the finances. She knows what she's doing. She's cheap as can be with some stuff, though. I have a heck of a time getting her to buy my lottery tickets."

—

Millions of butterflies fly across windswept desert for days. When I walk in the wash at daybreak I duck and swerve in my attempts to avoid them. I have never experienced a butterfly migration. Their flight is erratic. They flit and dart up and down, east and west, but their instinct carries them north. They do not investigate each blade of grass, each purple wildflower beckoning in the desert breeze. Some touch for a second and are then pulled back into the continual motion of fluttering wings.

I notice water inching down the wash, covering every ripple and cleft in the sand. The water moves erratically too, creeping like fog around mountains. I step up onto an embankment gouged out over time by flash floods and look at my surroundings. The sky is blue. Butterflies sweep past and their silken wings brush my bare arms and legs as they continue their relentless journey.

Steady noise comes from further up the wash. I cross to the other side and find a path through brush that takes me to the county road. The noise increases as I get closer to the canal. When I reach the construction site two huge pumps are emptying water from the gigantic pool.

All day I hear the murmur of pumps in the distance. I hear them when I make meals, when I clean up, when I stretch out for my afternoon rest, when I sit outside to read, when friends come to visit. As dusk settles I have become accustomed to the background noise and do not notice it any more until I notice silence.

In the morning I walk to the construction site. Men wearing hard hats are back at work in the bottom of the trench. Trucks move back and forth along the canal road. Heavy machines with giant tires stand ready. Work has resumed as if nothing had happened. It is rumoured that the canal project will take three years to complete. Beside the "Danger Keep Out" sign, there is now a wooden sign hammered into the ground that gives a name and phone number to call if any dust rises from this project.

—

When Dad died, he had been married to Mom three days shy of fifty-seven years. His affairs were in order. Although it was an emotional trip into the Bank of Commerce, where Dad had banked since arriving in Canada, it was a simple trip. We closed out his accounts and walked the cheques two blocks to the Bank of Montreal.

Mom chose the Bank of Montreal because the bus stop was outside the door. She had a savings account there but her music business was in the Royal Bank. We walked there and closed those accounts and walked the cheques a block and half back to the Bank of Montreal. She opened a new chequing account and invested Dad's money in a GIC. All her accounts were in both of our names. She wanted me to have signing authority. She wanted her affairs as tidy for me as Dad had left them for her.

Mom lived in their little home seven more years. Dad's clothes took up half the space in their bedroom closet all those seven years. His shaving supplies remained in the bathroom cupboard over the sink. His La-Z-Boy chair stayed in position in front of the television in the living room.

My brother, Mike, is custodian of Mom and Dad's photographs. He spent hours sitting on their couch, looking through albums when he visited. He loves the black and white photos from our childhood and our parents' childhoods. He offered to look after the photographs when Mom decided to live in The Manor. I boxed up Mom and Dad's albums, Granny and Grandad's albums and dozens of cartridges filled with slides and took them to Mike's home on a trip to Vancouver. I forgot the slide projector but Mike picked it up and took it home with him after one of his visits.

When he decided it was time to do something with the multitude of slides, he phoned me.

"I can't get this projector to work."

I laughed. "You're probably not doing it right."

"How do you do it?"

"You have to hit it and slam it."

"I'm not doing that."

"Well, that's what Mom and Dad did and it worked for them."

For what we are about to receive

I bake carrot cookies Saturday morning while Mom lies in her bed in extended care. I think her time is over. She had another stroke Tuesday morning that left her left hand and arm limp. She feels terrible. So do I. I feel terrible differently than she does. She is weak and sick. I am strong and well. I feel terrible that she can no longer feed herself, blow her nose or wipe her eyes. I feel terrible because she never wanted life to end like this.

—

"I don't want to linger," she said one day when we were sitting in her room in The Manor. We had returned from the November birthday party held in the dining room. Her and Bennett's party. The only two who had birthdays in November. Mom's eighty-ninth birthday. Mom and I shared her bingo cards. Mom won a game and picked a loonie from the tray of prizes. Perfume, soap, strings of beads, brooches and loonies littered the tray. Mom always chose money when she won.

"I don't want to linger," she repeated. "I want to go just like this." She swished her hands back and forth on top of one another. "I don't want to be a burden to you."

—

The recipe calls for a third of a cup of cooked, mashed carrots. I peel two carrots, cut and boil them. The recipe is from *Joy of Cooking*, a wedding gift from my sister-in-law, Hilary, in 1966. The spine of the book is broken and the pages yellow from age and use. Food is stuck on favourite recipes.

"Carrot Drop Cookies: A sophisticatedly flavoured soft tea cookie with an oil base." I have never taken the time to make these cookies. But this morning I make time because I want to bake and because I like the description. It reminds me of tea parties Mom had for groups of women friends in Nelson in the 1950s. Sometimes the tea party was for women who lived in the neighbourhood, sometimes for the United Church women and sometimes for women who volunteered for the Arthritis Society and the Hospital Auxiliary.

Mom worked hard to prepare for these tea parties. She got down on her hands and knees and washed and waxed the hardwood floors around the Persian carpets in the living room and dining room. She dusted her knick-knacks, bookcases, coffee tables, end tables, window ledges, buffet, china cabinet, dining room table legs, chair rungs. She vacuumed and tidied our normally slightly messy house.

I sat at the kitchen table with the silverware, the silver coffee service, silver loaf and cookie holders, a small can of Silvo and several clean, soft rags. My job was to clean and polish the silver while she scrubbed the house.

Once the house was clean, she baked for hours. Fancy, delicate cookies. Cookies that her children were not allowed to touch as they cooled on wire racks that covered every flat surface in the kitchen. She baked matrimonial cake and Nanaimo bars. There was always ample food in our home – pies and puddings for dessert, banana bread and carrot loaf, cookies with oatmeal and raisins – but the extravagant baking, the baking that didn't have anything in it that was good for you, was only baked for special occasions.

I carefully dried chinaware that Mom washed. Delicate cup and saucer sets each different from the other and small ornamental plates to hold the finest baking. I set them on top of the lacey, crocheted tablecloth centred on the dining room table. I set them beside the shining silverware.

When my children were growing up and we were invited to Mom and Dad's home for supper, the children complained when it was time to clean up. "Why does Grandma use so many dishes?" We ate off good china dishes, chipped after fifty years of use. Not all the cups and saucers matched anymore. Cups missing handles sat on window ledges holding small plants. Cracked bread and butter plates sat under slightly larger planters. Nothing was thrown away until it hit the floor and shattered into too many pieces to glue together.

Mom loved food and she loved the presentation of food. A silence cloth protected the dining room table and was covered with a white linen tablecloth. The table was set with the sharp edge of knives facing in towards the plate and the correct number of forks and spoons placed appropriately for the meal ahead. A bread and butter plate and glass was set at each place, as was a cloth napkin. When we

were young Dad taught us how to make "a baby in the cradle" with
our napkins. "Now, Ole, don't be making a mess of the table," Mom
complained from the kitchen as we rocked our babies back and forth.
A fresh flower centerpiece and candles held in elegant candlesticks
stretched down the middle of the table.

Food arrived from the kitchen in heated serving dishes and
platters. Heated plates were set in front of Dad. He carved the roast
and put meat onto each plate before passing the plate down the table.
China serving bowls were passed from hand to hand as we dished up
our own vegetables. Even if we didn't like spinach or squash, we had
to take a little and we had to eat it. No one lifted a fork until Mom sat
down at her place at the opposite end of the table from Dad, or before
the food was blessed. The five of us children took turns saying grace
during the week. On Sunday when Granny and Grandad came for
supper, Grandad said grace. It took a lot longer than the basic words
we said during the week. With Grandad it was more like a prayer.
He thanked the Lord for everything. My brothers made faces at me
from under their bowed heads trying to make me laugh. I had to keep
my eyes closed to avoid looking at them but even then it was hard
to smother the impulse to giggle. I was sent to the kitchen to eat by
myself if I misbehaved.

Mom occasionally said grace but Dad never did. When Mom
said grace she spoke the same words we children did, but the words
sounded sincere the way she spoke them. I think she said grace
every now and then to impress on us the meaning behind the words.
Perhaps we mumbled or spoke too quickly. I'm sure the words had
lost their meaning for us after countless repetitions and we had to be
reminded of their importance. "I'll say grace tonight," she announced.
We bowed our heads and we did not giggle.

The only time we heard Dad say grace was when we were out
for dinner and he was asked by the host to give the blessing. I always
felt nervous that he might not remember the words. He surprised me
when he recited the correct words and he surprised me more when he
improvised.

Only after grace was said, and after Mom picked up her fork and
ate her first mouthful, were we allowed to eat. Meals were raucous.
Teasing was handed out and dished back. As long as we sat up straight,

kept our feet flat on the floor, kept our elbows off the table, chewed with our mouths closed and didn't speak with our mouths full, we were allowed to express our opinions. Mealtimes were full of debate, discussion and laughter. We were not supposed to interrupt when someone else was talking. If whoever was talking paused for a breath or to ponder an idea, someone else jumped into that instant opening and gained the floor. I learned timing was everything if I wanted to add my thoughts.

When we could see all the flowers printed on the bottom of our English chinaware, the table was cleared. We took turns helping Mom make numerous trips back and forth from the kitchen. The rest of the family sat and waited for dessert to be brought to the table. There was bread pudding or pie, jelly or junket, cookies or cake, fresh fruit or canned fruit depending on the season. Dad counted cherries or strawberries as he spooned them into bowls so that we all got the same amount. If the count was unequal, he gave the extra to Mom. Sometimes he brought home a brick of ice cream for a treat. One of us chanted, "Ice cream, ice cream, we all scream for ice cream." We watched with eagle eyes as he made six marks with the knife before cutting and placing seven thin slices on clean plates. He handed them down the table. The first slice went to Mom.

After the meal was finished I asked Mom, "May I please be excused?" No one was allowed to leave the table without being excused. We often stayed long after the meal was finished and the debate wasn't. Mom and Dad drank their tea and Dad smoked his cigarette. If we lingered too long, and if Mom got impatient to start the cleanup, she announced, "You may all be excused from the table."

Mom's lifelong love of food included a love of eating together at family gatherings. Every visit centred on meals. In her senior years, when her sons and daughters-in-law, grandchildren, siblings, nieces and nephews came to Prince Rupert to visit, Mom was happiest when the family crowded around the table in her, or my, small kitchen. She didn't want to sit around talking all day. "Go out and do something. Go out and enjoy yourselves." She wanted to bake and prepare food for a gathering at suppertime. After Dad died, and after she recovered from her stroke, she was content to come to our home for supper and sit around our table surrounded by family who had travelled to see her.

She seldom took part in conversations that were as spirited as when we were growing up. She concentrated on the food, occasionally looking up and exclaiming, "My, this tastes good." Or, "Isn't it wonderful to be all together?"

Mom savoured all foods but if there was one that she relished more than any other, it was ice cream. Her spoon clanged the bottom of her bowl to get every last drop. When my brother, Mike, and his wife, Kathie, arrived on one of their visits, we were almost finished our meal, when Kathie got the giggles. Both Mom and Mike were scraping the bottom of their ice cream bowls with determination and the rest of us had not noticed the noise coming from their bowls.

"I'm sorry," Kathie stuttered between uncontrollable giggles. "Now I know where Mike gets it from. He doesn't even know he does it."

—

I mash the cooked carrots and add them to the other ingredients. I do not add the four tablespoons of white raisins mentioned in the recipe. Mom seldom has her teeth in anymore. She has steadily been losing weight and her teeth don't fit right. I will take two cookies with me when I visit in the afternoon. She will enjoy a cookie but she likes to share her treats with me. She has never liked eating alone.

I visit every day, late in the afternoon. I read to her for a half an hour until her supper tray arrives. Three of the four women in the room need help with their meals. I go to a closet and bring out four paper bibs. I place one around each woman's neck. I help Mom with her meal. Staff or family members help the other women.

Mom's meal is pureed. She opens her mouth like a baby bird. I place a small spoonful of meat into Mom's mouth. Eating is a slow process. She has difficulty swallowing so every spoonful takes a while. She opens her mouth for vegetables but will not open her mouth for potatoes. "I don't want any potatoes," she says.

"Don't you like them?" I ask.

"It's not that I don't like them. I just don't want any more potatoes."

"You don't have to eat them. I guess you've eaten enough potatoes in your life."

"I certainly have."

I scrape gravy off the potatoes and onto the meat and vegetables. Mom likes gravy. The kitchen staff know this and dollop an extra spoonful over her meal. They also know her love of ice cream and as she gets weaker, and more of her food is returned to the kitchen untouched, a Dixie cup of ice cream is added to her tray. She will always eat a few mouthfuls.

Mike arrives after I tell him of Mom's latest stroke, the stroke that has rendered her left hand and arm useless, the stroke that has left her unable to do anything for herself. He wants to help. There isn't much he can do, but just being with us helps both Mom and me. He recognizes our plight. He supports our attempt for dignity and decency. He brings remembrance of a happy childhood and a time when Mom was strong and vibrant. He confirms our love of family.

He asks, "What can I do?"

"Do you want to help Mom with her supper?"

"O.K."

I show him where the bibs are kept and suggest he get one for each of the four women in the room. He needs no more instruction. I watch as one by one he tenderly lifts each head off a pillow and slips a bib over an old woman's head. He is so gentle. Sweet smiles are his reward. Mom says, "Thank you, Michael."

When supper arrives, Mike lifts the warming lid off the plate, picks up a spoon and fills it with pureed food. "I bet you never thought the tables would be turned like this when I was a baby," he teases.

"No, I certainly did not," she replies. She opens her mouth and Mike's mouth opens, too, as he slips the spoon into her mouth. Her eyes never leave his face.

"That's enough, dearie," she says after a few spoonfuls. "I don't want any more."

"Does that mean I can eat your ice cream?" Mike asks.

She smiles, "No, it doesn't."

"I thought you were full."

"I'm not that full."

Mike takes the lid off the Dixie cup and slowly feeds Mom her ice cream until his exaggerated scraping of the spoon against the empty container makes us laugh.

"Thank you very much, Michael. It is good of you to help me."

Goodbyes are always difficult and on the last day of Mike's visit, after he has grown accustomed to the world of extended care, the world of patients and their families, the world of staff with their variety of personalities, he leaves this routine with which he has become familiar. Mom's words to Mike are brave, "Goodbye, Michael. Take care of yourself. Give my love to Kathie and to Melissa and Shelley. Don't worry about me. I'm fine and I'm well taken care of."

Mike hugs her. "I love you, Mom."

Her sobs arrive and she sputters, "Just go. Just go."

We back out of the room not wanting to leave her like this but knowing we have to leave sooner or later and we don't want to go through this again. We are both wiping our eyes as we go down in the elevator. "I hate this part," Mike says.

"I hate it, too, Mike. I have to remind myself what a nurse in The Manor told me a long time ago when Bill and I were leaving for a few months. I'd gone to the nursing station to ask the head nurse to keep an eye on Mom, that she was really upset. The nurse told me that it was good for Mom to have a good cry, that it lowered her blood pressure."

"Are you trying to tell me that I should feel good about leaving Mom like this?"

"If it will make you feel any better."

Despite numerous attempts by the physiotherapy department, Mom's ability to move her left hand and fingers does not improve. Her hand and arm are put in a brace so they will not curl up like her right hand did after her first stroke thirteen years ago. A holder is fabricated for her books and she is given a rubber finger to turn pages. She is instructed to do special exercises four times a day.

She does not like the brace. She does not want to read. She will not do the exercises.

"Are you in pain?" I ask.

"No, dearie. I'm not in any pain. The brace is uncomfortable, that's all. I don't know what's the matter with me. I don't feel like doing anything anymore."

"Don't you want to read? It's such a long day for you if you just sit in your chair or lay in your bed."

"I've tried reading but it's too much of a bother with the new contraptions."

"Would you like me to read to you?" I ask.

"If you'd like to. That would be very nice."

I look in her bottom drawer and sort through the books. There is a new book her daughter-in-law, Carol, sent to her. It's the story of a woman who has had a stroke and is ready to give up when she meets and falls in love with the carpenter who is working on the house next door. I have told my family that Mom loves to read and she loves to read romantic novels. Anything full of love and sex will get her undivided attention. I start reading and within pages I realize I'm in trouble.

I drop the book into my lap. "Mom, there's a pretty graphic sex scene coming up. How will you be with that?"

"I don't know about you, but I'll be fine."

I pick up the book and continue reading. I eliminate words and then full sentences. I am not comfortable reading the description of how the carpenter is making the woman aware of her sexuality. Nor am I comfortable reading details of their lovemaking in a room with three other women, their visitors, and staff coming into the room. The chapter ends more quickly than it should have.

"We'll read another chapter tomorrow."

"That will be wonderful, dearie. Thank you very much."

I arrive at the hospital the next afternoon to read a chapter of the book and to help Mom with her supper. She is not in her room. I look in the kitchen, the living room, the hallways. I cannot find her. It is Sunday and there is only a skeleton staff on duty. I go to the nursing station and Charles, the nurse on duty, sees me. "Nancy," he says. "I've been trying to reach you. I left a message on your answering machine. Your mother is not responding. We have moved her into palliative care."

For three days Mom lies in bed without responding. Staff offer to bring a bed for me so I can stay with Mom. "Thank you," I say, "but no thank you." I know I will not get any sleep with the noise of the nursing station across the hallway. Phones and call bells ring constantly and there is a steady stream of people coming and going at all hours. I know, too, that Mom responds to routine so I arrive mid-afternoon, sit and hold her hand, and tell her about my day. Then I read a chapter of the love story. Now that we are alone and she appears to be unconscious, I read every word out loud. The love affair is blooming and so are the descriptions of their lovemaking. I stop reading occasionally to swab Mom's lips with a wet sponge on a stick. She opens her mouth and grasps the sponge. She only loosens her grip when the moisture is out of the sponge. I dunk the sponge in her water jug and repeat the motion on her lips. Again she opens her mouth and grasps the sponge. I continue to give her water this way until she will not open her mouth any more. I sit down, pick up the book and resume reading.

Bill arrives and as he comes through the door he hears me reading a passionate sentence. "What's going on in here?" he asks in a loud voice.

Mom's eyes open. "Hello, Bill," she says in a whisper.

There is almost a giddiness among the staff, visitors, volunteers, even some of the residents who arrive in the palliative care room in their wheelchairs. All are happy that Dorothy is making a comeback. She smiles and thanks each person who visits or cares for her.

I continue my afternoon routine with Mom although now I go back to reading my censored version of the story. When her supper tray arrives I put the book away in a drawer in the bedside table. She only eats a small amount and she eats slowly.

The second day after her amazing recovery, her friend, Fran, arrives for a visit at the same time as Mom's supper tray arrives. "Oh," Fran says, "perhaps you would like me to come back later."

"Oh, no," Mom and I say simultaneously.

"Would you like to help Mom with her supper?" I ask.

"You don't mind?"

"Of course not. She would love a visit with you."

I put on my coat and kiss Mom goodbye. "See you tomorrow."

"Goodbye, dearie, and thank you for everything."

As I leave the room I hear Fran ask Mom if she would like a prayer before she eats.

"Yes, please, Fran. That would be lovely."

I hesitate outside the door and listen as Fran starts, "Thank you, Lord, for this food and thank you for taking care of Dorothy..." Her voice fades as I walk towards the elevator.

Mom's affection for her friends has never wavered. They add a dimension to her life that only true friendship can. They were a large part of Mom's life when her passion was music and the church. They were her contemporaries, and a true bond of friendship formed that held firm throughout Mom's diminishing capacities. Mom loves them dearly and they love her. Mom's friends, and the minister from the United Church, fill a void that my four brothers and I created when our faith in the church disappeared in teenage years. When Vince and Carol's five children were growing up they had to say grace at suppertime. Vince said it wasn't for religious reasons. He thought children should learn to be thankful for food that is purchased, prepared and eaten daily.

At Shirley's home, their three young children take turns saying grace at suppertime. "For the food we are about to receive, we are truly thankful."

I do not say grace with Mom the last year of her life. I feed her almost every supper and she never once complains. She gets weaker and weaker but never fails to say, "Thank you."

Both Mom and I thank the kitchen staff every time a tray of food appears in front of her. Perhaps Mom says a silent prayer before she eats. But I never think of it. Suppertime is a jovial time in the ward. Lots of laughter and teasing as staff cajole the old women to have "one more mouthful." It is not unlike our childhood suppertimes. A gathering for fellowship and good cheer.

—

When I visit Shirley and her husband, Mario, in the Okanagan, I love to bake and make meals for the family. Often one of my three grandchildren sits on the counter beside me or stands on a chair pushed up against the counter. I make oatmeal raisin cookies one afternoon. Another afternoon I look in Shirley's *Joy of Cooking* for a recipe for rolled cookies. Four-year-old Allison and I make dough and she kneels on her chair at the kitchen table with the rolling pin and cookie cutters. She rolls the dough with all her might, not wanting any help from her Nana. She leans on the different cookie cutters, making stars and diamonds and squares, and lifts and places the cookies on cookie sheets. She sprinkles coloured sparkles on some, chocolate beads on others, and presses them into the cookies. I gather bits and pieces of leftover dough, form another ball and give it to Allison to roll and cut more cookies. We have cookies cooling on wire racks on the kitchen counter when her two brothers arrive home after school.

I make rhubarb crisp from rhubarb that my grandsons, Michael and Daniel, pulled from the garden last summer. Rhubarb that Shirley cut and froze. We will have the crisp for dessert with ice cream.

I roast two small chickens in the oven. I whip potatoes, mash yams with butter and brown sugar, steam carrots and peas, stir the gravy. Shirley makes the stovetop dressing her family likes. I have never made stovetop dressing. Like Mom, I put the dressing in the bird.

When the family gathers for supper, Shirley asks, "Mom, would you like to say grace tonight?"

"O.K.," I answer. I bow my head and begin my childhood prayer, "For what we are about to receive ...."

Six-year-old Daniel interrupts, "Nana, that's not the way it goes!"

Perhaps he is nervous for me the way I was nervous for Dad all those many years ago. Nervous that Dad couldn't remember the words or wouldn't say grace right.

Shirley signals to him to be quiet, her finger against her lips.

I begin again, slowly, "For what we are about to receive...." I think of Mom and how she said the same grace her children said but with more meaning than we managed. "... may the Lord make us truly thankful, Amen."

*T*he years have been kind to you," said an old friend I had not seen for many years. I want to repeat that to the middle-aged man who offers me his seat on a crowded 98 B-Line bus from Vancouver to Richmond. I want to protest, to say that I'm not so old he should give up his seat for me. I want to protest but I don't. It's at least a thirty-minute ride from the corner of 41st Avenue and Granville to the Richmond Centre. It's pouring with rain. Everyone crammed in the bus has a dripping umbrella, and dampness spreads from pant legs and shoes to misted windows. Beads of moisture form patterns as they slither down the panes. Occasionally someone lifts an arm and wipes a window with a jacket sleeve but it does not clear water from glass. It is difficult for me to stand, my arthritic hand latched onto an overhead strap, and avoid wet umbrellas banging against my legs.

"Thank you," I offer in exchange for the seat. The same words I uttered when told how kind the years had been. I think the other passengers want to say thank you, too, to the man now standing. Now that we no longer stand face to face they do not have to smell my boozy breath.

I transferred onto this bus from a 41st Avenue bus that I caught in Kerrisdale after drinking two pints of beer with my son, Clint. We like to have Happy Hour together. When I housesit for my brother-in-law in Richmond, I often take the bus into Vancouver to meet Clint at the school on Granville Street where he teaches art. We drive to his apartment in Kerrisdale and walk to a cozy pub in the heart of the district. We never tire of discussing art and artists and the inspiration we get from looking at other artists' work. Two pints is never enough when we are together but it is all we allow ourselves when I have to take the bus back to Richmond.

It wasn't raining when we left Clint's apartment and walked to the pub, but it was coming down in buckets when we left the pub. We huddled under my umbrella and ran the block to the bus stop. Rain streamed off my umbrella and soaked our outside shoulders. When the 41st Avenue bus pulled up I kissed Clint on the cheek and stood in line to get on the bus. I turned to look at him running down the street, his long legs carrying his lanky body through sheets of rain.

I had to stand on the 41st Avenue bus. I was pleased when the driver called out, "Granville." I could not see what stop we were at through the fogged up windows. Half the people got off to transfer to the 98 B-Line bus now waiting at the intersection for the red light to turn green. The display on the front of that bus showed, "Sorry. Bus Full." Some people crowded together and waited under the covered bench for the next bus. Others, including myself, ran through puddles and stood at the bus stop in the pounding rain. When the light turned green the full bus passed through the intersection, splashed through a stream of water alongside the curb and stopped. I stepped up into the bus. "Thank you," I said to the bus driver who had decided he could cram in a few more passengers. A recorded "Please move to the back of the bus" prompted people to wiggle closer together allowing room for a few more passengers who followed and propelled me into the mob.

Now that I have settled into the seat the gentleman offered me, my body sways to the motion of the bus swerving from lane to lane. My wet thighs and shoulders rest against an old, fat man on one side of me and a young, fat woman on the other. We sway together, none of us trying to escape the touch of a stranger. Except for the dampness and the mingling of perfume, smoke and occasionally a whiff of an unwashed body, the closeness is comfortable. The young woman is listening to music on an iPod. Her eyes are closed and her body keeps beat to the rhythm pulsing into her ears. The old man drifts in and out of sleep. His head falls forward then his neck jerks his head upright again. Sometimes his own snorting wakes him and his eyes look startled like an animal's eyes caught in a car's headlights.

Mostly I enjoy public transportation in a big city, watching as people enter and exit my bus-bound world. But there is one segment of the population missing. The old folk who lie in hospital beds or extended care, too old or disabled to engage with people in their communities. This segment is hidden, not intentionally, not like lepers cast aside and hidden in earlier days, but still mostly invisible. Unless you have a parent or grandparent who lives to old age and you visit occasionally, you would not know that there are those who continue to live but are unable to use the public transportation of life.

Such was Mom's last year.

I don't know why she clung to life, why she didn't get off at the end of the line. I don't know why she chose to sit on the bus, in the station, until it started its run again the next morning. Over and over again, day after day, week after week, month after month. I don't know why she chose this route. Maybe she did it for me. Maybe she wanted me to experience the cycle of life.

There is no defining moment that I can think of when we entered this last phase of her life. I photographed her on her ninety-second birthday, sitting in her wheelchair, dressed in a new outfit her daughter-in-law, Carol, sent for her birthday. The black and white photo sits on a bookshelf in our living room. It is a lovely photo of Mom. It is hard to believe she was ninety-two when the photo was taken. Her skin looks smooth, unwrinkled, a benefit of her extra weight. Her eyes look clear, intelligent, a benefit from keeping her mind busy with music, books, magazines and crossword puzzles. Her hands rest on her legs. Her right hand is curled up, the result of her stroke when she was eighty years old. Her left hand flat, her wedding band and engagement ring worn thin from constant wear since 1932. Her watch, tight around her wrist, was part of her daily attire.

I did not photograph Mom on her ninety-third birthday. But the image I have is clear in my mind. She was lying in her bed in extended care. She wore a pale blue hospital gown. Her teeth were in a glass on her bedside table. Her glasses and hearing aid were in their cases beside her teeth. She looked old, frail and tired. At this point it was hard for me to believe she was still alive. She had suffered several small strokes that slowly diminished all her capabilities. Several times I sat beside her bed for hours expecting the current crisis to be the last crisis.

But here we were, celebrating another birthday, only this time we were not partying with other residents and old friends in the living room. Music drifted down hallways and we heard muffled voices singing familiar tunes. Beth, the activity coordinator, left the party with several staff members and arrived in Mom's room carrying a cake with candles blazing. When they surrounded her, singing, "Happy birthday, dear Dorothy," tears streamed down her face.

"Dorothy!" Beth exclaimed, "Why are you crying? This is a happy occasion!"

Mom tried to say "Thank you" but her tears turned to sobs. As each staff member gave her a birthday hug, they came away with tears glistening in their eyes. When they returned to the party, I wiped my eyes and Mom's eyes. I gave her a few mouthfuls of her cake before eating my piece. I walked to the kitchen and got her a Dixie cup of ice cream from the fridge.

"Aren't you going to have one?" she asked.

"No, thanks, Mom. The cake was enough for me."

"It was delicious, wasn't it?"

"Yes, it was. It was a real treat."

"I don't know what got into me. I don't know why I acted like that."

"It's all right. It's a sentimental day for you."

"That's no reason to behave like that."

"Tears are good for you. They cleanse your eyes."

There were days when she felt good and staff got her up and dressed and into her wheelchair. On those days I took her outside to feel the breeze on her face and the warmth of the sun on her body. Every afternoon I read a chapter of whatever novel we were reading at the time. If we were outside I sat on a big flat rock with Mom beside me in her wheelchair. In retrospect, I think those afternoons provided some of my finest moments with Mom. How lucky I was to have time in my life to read a chapter of a book almost every day for a year with my aging mother. Often I would lift my eyes from the page to glance at Mom and she was looking at me with tears in her eyes. I would touch her arm or stoke her hand or move a whiff of white hair from her forehead.

"Are you O.K., Mom?" I'd ask.

"I'm fine, dearie," she'd answer.

"Are you getting cold?"

"A little bit."

"Do you want to go inside?"

"No, not yet. Let's finish the chapter."

When I closed the book at the end of the chapter, Mom said, "Thank you, dearie. That's really something." Or, "Thank you, dearie. That's very interesting." A comment always followed her expression of gratitude.

The weather was cold and blustery when we started the book *Clara Callan*. We did not go outside. I pushed Mom down the hallway to the small visitors' room with its comfortable couch and chair, lamps and tables. Within a day or two we had company for the reading. Residents who were mobile joined us. One man waited outside the elevator in his wheelchair every afternoon. "Oh, good," he said. "You're here." He wheeled himself down the hallway to wait for me to bring Mom and *Clara Callan*. There were other regulars who waited in the room for us, too, and there was one old woman who would not come into the room but sat in her wheelchair outside the door, her whole body leaning towards the open doorway and her head tilted to one side.

I read every word of that book out loud. I think the story transported the old folk back to their early adulthood in the thirties, to their adventures, their misadventures. One day when the visitors' room was occupied by a family grieving the death of their father, I wheeled Mom down to the kitchen where we sat at a table by the window. Our book club followed us down the hallway and circled the table. There were others in the room: residents with visitors sharing a cup of tea and home baking, staff helping, coming and going. I started to read. The murmur of the others in the room did not disturb us. I was unaware that the chapter I was about to read contained a rape scene. I sensed the tension of the story and felt sick inside as the words came out of my mouth. The circle tightened as heads leaned forward to catch every word. The everyday noises in the kitchen ceased. An old man's wife who was visiting him started to talk. "Shut up," he demanded. "I'm listening."

I will never forget the silence that followed the end of that chapter. It was like we had all been violated. Mom did not say, "Wasn't that something." She didn't even say, "Thank you."

I sat with Mom until her supper arrived. I helped her with her meal then I wheeled her to her room. I put my coat on.

"Is it time for you to go?" Mom asked.

"Yes. It's time to start supper at home."

I hugged her and kissed her goodbye. "I love you, Mom," I said.

"Thank you, dearie."

I turned to leave. "Nancy," she said.

I looked back.

"I love you."

It wouldn't have had such a profound effect on me if those were words spoken often or easily by Mom. I never expected to hear the words and the few times in her life when she did tell me she loved me, I thought there was something the matter. That maybe she was sick. Maybe she thought she was dying. I remember one time when Mom was in The Manor, and Bill and I were in California for the winter. I phoned Mom every Sunday morning between ten and eleven. She answered her phone after the first ring. I knew she expected my call and sat there waiting for it. One Sunday morning the phone rang and rang. Mom did not answer.

When I returned to our campsite Bill asked, "Everything O.K.?"

"No," I answered. "I think something is the matter. Mom did not answer her phone."

"I'll drive you to town later and you can try again."

When she answered my call later in the afternoon, a wave of relief swept over me. I loved my winter travels with Bill. But it was never easy leaving her, never knowing if I would see her alive again when I said, "Goodbye."

Mom answered after the first ring. "I was hoping you'd phone again," she said.

"Are you all right?" I asked.

"I am now," she said. "I wasn't very good last night. I kept throwing up and someone got worried about me. They took me to the hospital and I spent the night there. I told them I had to get back, that I was expecting a call, but they didn't get me back in time. I heard the phone ringing as I got to my door but by the time I unlocked it and got to the phone, you had hung up."

"Are you sure you're O.K.?"

"Yes, dearie. As far as I know, I'm all right."

Our conversations were never long. I asked her how she was and she answered, "Just the same as last week." She asked me if I was having a good time. I answered, "Yes, I'm having a wonderful time." She kept a notepad by her phone and jotted down anything she wanted to remember to tell me. When she finished she said, "We better hang up now. This call is costing you money."

This conversation lasted several minutes longer than it usually did. She sounded fine, she had lots to tell me. I knew she was finished when she said, "Well, we better hang up now. This call is costing you a lot of money."

I replied with my usual comment, "Don't worry about it. It's Bill's money."

"Oh, in that case we'll talk longer," she teased.

"I'll phone next Sunday morning, same time, same station."

"O.K., dearie. Goodbye for now."

"Goodbye, Mom. I love you."

"Thank you, dearie."

This was the way all our phone calls ended. Except this time. After Mom said, "Thank you, dearie," she added, "I love you."

Bill was waiting for me in his truck. He thought I had received bad news when he saw me walk towards him. "What's the matter?" he asked.

"She told me she loved me. She's never said that in all the years I've been phoning."

I thought about it off and on all week. I thought she must be sicker than she was letting on. I thought it was her way of telling me something. I never thought she was just saying she loved me, that wasn't her style. Since I was a child, Mom expected a high standard of behaviour. When her standard was met she did not say, "I love you." She said, "Thank you."

By the time I was reading the final chapters of *Clara Callan*, Mom was seldom in her wheelchair. I sat on a chair beside her bed and the regular listeners crowded around us. I had a difficult time reading the final chapter and the epilogue. All the emotion of the story gathered in my throat and created a lump that threatened to erupt. I often stopped reading, cleared my throat and took a few deep breaths before I resumed reading. For the final page I could not stop the tears. I had to stop and wipe my eyes in order to see the page. I could not see the tears of others until the book was closed and my eyes were wiped. We laughed together, finding humour in the collective release of emotion.

I got a phone call at home one morning from one of the nurses in extended care advising me there was a bed available by the window in another room. "Would you mind if we moved your mom so that she could have a view?"

"Did you ask Mom?" I inquired.

"Yes."

"What did she say?"

"She said yes."

"If Mom wants to move that's fine with me. I know she would love the view."

"Great. We don't like to move anyone without the family's permission. Some people get really upset."

When I visited Mom later that day, I understood why some people got really upset. The four-bed ward that had been Mom's home for three years was like living in a small town. Moving to a room down the hallway was like moving to another country where people spoke a different language. Mom's neighbours in her old room had been lucid, no matter how old, frail or disabled their bodies had become. There was a familiar pattern to every day. We knew the women and we knew their families. Every day when I arrived the first thing I did, after kissing Mom and saying hello to her and anyone else in the room, was to take her water jug and Suzy's to the kitchen and fill them with fresh ice and water. Mom loved cold water and Suzy loved the attention. A comradeship had developed between the residents, their families and staff. It was like one big family who knew one another's quirks and routines.

Life in the room down the hall was totally different. Gone were the calm, quiet afternoons. I have to admit that I was upset for a while after Mom's move. I wished we were back in her little corner against the wall instead of beside the window in this noisy, boisterous room. I could hear the women before I got through the door.

"Nurse! Nurse! Nurse!" Emily yelled.

"Mom? Dad? Is that you?" Georgette asked every time Emily hollered or every time someone entered the room.

In the bed across from Mom, Millie wept. It wasn't that her weeping was loud, it was just so sad to hear.

I did not complain, nor did Mom. I greeted her the same as always, then picked up her water jug. I walked to her old room, greeted the people there, and picked up Suzy's water jug. I took Suzy's jug back to her before returning to Mom's room. "What took you so long?" Mom asked.

"I took fresh water to Suzy."

"Oh. How is she?"

"Fine. How are you?"

"Just the same as yesterday."

"Your view is lovely."

"It is, isn't it? I'm really enjoying it."

It was nice for Mom to see blue sky or moody clouds, to know the changing seasons by the length of daylight. It was nice she had natural light pouring over her bed during the day instead of artificial lighting. It was nice to have the window ledge for potted plants and bouquets of flowers. Staff cranked her bed up so she was high enough to see the view. They tilted the top of her bed forward, then lifted her head and shoulders and wedged pillows around her so she could see the world outside.

I adjusted to the change of lifestyle. I brought Georgette fresh water and held the straw to her lips so she could take a sip. I tucked Emily's teddy bear into her arms when she hollered or banged her hairbrush on the metal bars that held her in bed. Millie stopped weeping as soon as I started reading. I got to know and love the old women and their families. Nothing was normal or predictable. Some days were awful, some days were fun. Some days Millie's husband brought his accordion. He played and sang familiar songs to which I could sing along. Staff knew the individual characteristics of the women and teased and touched them and did their best to make them comfortable and happy. Family members arrived with grandchildren and pets, visitors brought flowers and baking, volunteers made tea, played the piano, took wheelchair-bound residents for walks, helped with meals, hung quilts on the walls, helped staff with parties and activities.

Although I never knew what I was going to see or hear from one day to the next, there was one constant to each and every day. I read a chapter of a book out loud.

By the time Mom and I were reading *Mrs. Mike*, life was simple for us. I walked to the hospital mid-afternoon, sat with Mom and read. I waited for supper to arrive and helped her with her meal. After a hug and kiss, I walked to the staircase, descended four flights of stairs and walked home. This routine took on a life of its own. It was totally separate from the rest of my life. It absorbed most of my conscious moments and affected most of my decisions. Although I continued to share my life with Bill, take part in my children's and grandchildren's lives and keep friendships and correspondence intact, I planned my life around my daily visit with Mom. I took my energy to the hospital every day and most days I left it there. When I think of the value of family and friends in that difficult year, it was the ability of loved ones to understand, and to give of themselves when I had nothing left to give back.

In the simplicity of Mom's life, she was totally dependent on others for her everyday care. She was washed and bathed and had her diapers changed by staff. She was given sustenance regularly. Her position in bed was changed every few hours. Her hair was combed, Kleenex held to nose, vomit cleaned up. There was nothing Mom could do for herself except to swallow and void.

But there was a lot she could do, and did, for others. She had a smile for everyone with whom she came in contact. She was kind and loving to family, friends, visitors and staff. She appreciated any attempt to make her life comfortable. She expressed gratitude constantly.

She was usually lying on her left side, facing the door, when I arrived. Her eyes caught mine as soon as I entered the room. I was greeted with a smile. I acknowledged the demands of the other women, "Just a minute. I'll be with you in a minute," but I went to Mom first. Only after our greeting did I return to deal with whoever was unhappy or needy. Sometimes all it took was to fluff a pillow and tuck bed covers in around arms and legs. Sometimes it was just to hold an outstretched hand. Sometimes I had to say, "I'll find someone to help you."

Georgette said, "Your mom is taking all your power."

I did what I could before setting a chair beside Mom and beginning another chapter of whatever book we were reading. I read nine books out loud the last year of Mom's life. *Mrs. Mike* garnered an audience. Visitors did not leave until the end of the chapter. It was a sentimental favourite for me. It was the first book from the adult section of the library that I read. It was the first adult love story I read. It was the first tragedy I read.

Desiree was my grandfather's book. His name, Robert H. Thornton, is written on the first page inside the book. Mom gave me the book to read as a teenager. I gave it to my daughter to read when she was a teenager. Shirley has the book now. I'm sure she will give it to Allison to read when she is a teenager.

Jake and the Kid was the staff's favourite. They could find laundry to fold and closets to tidy, residents to pamper and water jugs to fill until the end of the chapter.

I loved Margaret Laurence's memoir *Dance on the Earth*. Her relationships with her three mothers and the women who brought meaning to her life were particularly poignant to me under the circumstances.

My friend, Heather, lent me *The Judge's Wife* and we read about pioneer days in Victoria and experiences in the San Francisco earthquake in 1906 and the resulting fires that swept through the city.

By the time I was reading *A Small and Charming World*, Mom slept through most of the chapters. Sometimes I stopped reading. I thought I'd wait until she woke so she wouldn't miss the story. But when I stopped reading she opened her eyes. When I resumed reading her eyes closed again.

As the days rolled into weeks, and the weeks into months, Mom grew weaker and weaker. Her once hefty body gradually became thin. Her once unlined skin sagged and wrinkled. There were days when her voice was barely audible when she greeted me.

I went for her ice water and returned to put the straw to her lips. She could barely muster the energy to draw water from the straw. After a few tries she would finally get some water into her mouth only to choke on it in her attempt to swallow. Her feeble coughs sounded pathetic. Still she managed to whisper, "Oh, that's cold. Thank you, dearie."

I kept chocolate peppermint sticks in her dresser drawer. If she was awake when I read to her, I broke a small piece off and slipped it into her mouth. She smiled when her taste buds caught the flavour.

There were other days, the days that upset me more than any others, when she became animated. She had lively conversations with the ceiling, the walls. She waved her feeble arms and struggled against the bars that held her into bed. Staff warned me when they saw me step out of the elevator and walk past the nursing station, "Your mom isn't with us today." I knew then that she had entered one of her goofy periods, as I called them, and I found this part of life's cycle the most upsetting to witness. She was surprised and thrilled to see me. "Mother! When did you get back? My, it's good to see you! I can't get over you being here! How did you get here?"

I tried to be playful. I knew she was happy having her mother, or at times her sister, Joyce, with her. I tried to respond with cheer. "It's wonderful to see you, too! How are you?" But my playfulness didn't lift my heavy heart.

When I read she couldn't keep still and quiet. She thought she was misbehaving and giggled. She covered her mouth with her hand and tried to hide her glee. "I'm sorry, Mother. I'm just so happy to see you." When I left it was painful for us both. She cried, "Please, Mother, don't leave me! Take me with you! I promise to behave myself!"

The spells usually lasted two days. I got to know they preceded small strokes. After a couple of days of nonstop babble and childish behaviour, she crashed. There were a couple more days of not responding, and then the struggle back to sanity and a weakness that was even more pronounced than I would have thought possible.

It was during one of the returns to the sane world, when I went back to the hospital in the evening, when I thought Mom would not recover, when I sat beside her bed and held her hand and swabbed her lips with water, that Georgette called out to me in the darkness of the room. The only light came from the light in the hallway that poured through the open doorway and spilled across the floor. When I heard Georgette, I got up and went to her bedside. She reached for my hand. "You are very lucky to see the sorry side," she said.

━

The 98 B-Line bus crosses the Arthur Lang Bridge over the Fraser River and stops at Airport Station. Several people leave the bus. At every stop through Richmond more people get off. When we reach Richmond Centre everyone leaves the bus. This is the end of the line. Now the bus driver will drive around the block and start his run into Vancouver all over again. At this point, I can wait to transfer to a

Number Three bus or walk two miles to my brother-in-law's home. It is still raining but not heavily. It is spitting, as Mom would say. So many things remind me of her: an expression, a gesture, a piece of music.

Details of her final year blur with the passage of time. I'm left with a sensation, an intimate knowledge that makes it possible for me to be comfortable with old people. To understand their frustration, their discomfort, their joy, their pride. To open doors and hold them open when I see people with walkers or wheelchairs. To take baking to seniors who live in their own homes. To touch, hug, listen. I try to bring my knowledge or compassion to others who struggle with the complications of aging parents.

I thought after Mom died that I would continue to read to the old folk in extended care. But I have not been able to do that. I finished the last book and stopped reading two days before Mom died. She had lost the ability to swallow a few days earlier. The nurse in charge told me, "Your mom isn't doing well." Doctor Coburn saw me at the hospital. I said, "Mom's having a hard time." He answered, "I think she is near the end, Nancy."

Her eyes never left my face when I read the last chapter to her. Her eyes stayed open the whole time. I asked her if she was feeling any better. She whispered, "The same."

"Are you in any pain?"

"No."

I could feel her bony shoulders through her cotton nightgown when I hugged her goodbye. "I love you, Mom."

Tears slipped down her cheeks. She tried to say goodbye but I don't think she had the strength.

I went back in the evening and sat with her but she never woke again. The next morning she was moved into palliative care. My brother, Mike, arrived that morning. When we got to her room I greeted her as always with a hug and kiss and said, "Mom! Mom! Mike is here!" Her eyes opened and then they closed.

Her eyes opened one more time later that morning. They opened when Gilbert, one of Mom's nurses, came into the room. "Dorothy! What are you doing in here?" Her eyes opened and then they closed.

She lingered, sleeping peacefully, for two days. Long enough for her close friends, and the old and the new ministers from the church, to have a prayer with her and to say goodbye.

It seemed fitting that Sumitra, Mom's old neighbour from Ninth Avenue whose children took piano lessons from her, the nurse who welcomed Mom to extended care, was the nurse on duty the night Mom died. She came into the room throughout the evening and with soft words and professional knowledge brought comfort to Mike and me.

We stayed with Mom until the end. If death can be beautiful, then Mom's death was beautiful. She was quiet and still. Her breaths came further and further apart until they didn't come any more. The drapes were open to the night. The lights were dimmed in the room. One of Mom's organ tapes played softly in her small tape deck.

—

When I get off the bus at Richmond Centre, I stand and try to decide whether to walk or wait for the Number Three bus. I put my umbrella up and look around. Darkness has settled over the city and lights reflect and shimmer on wet pavement. My eyes spot Bill scurrying around puddles of water that have pooled up on the shopping centre's parking lot. I watch him, his hands in his pockets, his baseball cap low on his head keeping raindrops off his glasses. His shoulders scrunch his neck into his jacket collar as if that will stop the rain from hitting him. Once again Clint has phoned Bill and told him I'm on my way. He has driven to meet my bus like he has done so many times before. I walk towards him. He smiles when he sees me. I tuck my arm through his, draw him close and hold the umbrella over our heads.

Acknowledgements

*M*om would have loved her evening memorial service at the United Church. The warmth of candlelight and the beauty of calla lilies stirred childhood memories in my heart. Dad bought Mom a potted Easter lily every Easter and a potted poinsettia every Christmas. But for special occasions he bought her calla lilies. I remember the joy his gift brought. She loved the calla lily plant. She planted the gift in her elaborate garden and tended it with loving care.

The real tribute to Mom, aside from the kind and loving words, was the music. Judy Rea, the woman to whom Mom had given lessons, played the organ. Members of the community choir joined the regular members of the United Church choir and led the congregation singing hymns that Mom's church friends had chosen. The choir sang the anthem, *Jesu, Joy of Man's Desiring.* I thanked the choir after the service. I said, "You sang like angels." One of the choir members replied, "We were looking down on one."

His kind words recognized my relationship with Mom. And talking with several members of the fourth floor family who came to the service was sentimental whether they were family members of residents or hospital staff. We had all lost a member of the family when Mom died. The inevitability of death of old residents who lingered, and the recent death of others, put our emotions close to the surface. One of Mom's nurses hugged me and said, "I'm a leaky bucket at these things."

The thought of finishing a book without a special thank you to all the medical staff who cared for my parents is impossible. I want to express my gratitude to Doctor Coburn, Mary, Angenita, Eva, all the nurses, aides, physiotherapists, kitchen staff, cleaners, receptionists, ambulance and emergency personnel, everyone who gave competent, loving and compassionate care to Mom and Dad in their home, Acropolis Manor and the third and fourth floors of Prince Rupert Regional Hospital. I would love to name you all, to thank you personally, but there is the danger of forgetting someone's name. I will not, however, forget the care you gave my folks. I am fortunate to have brushed shoulders with so many wonderful people. Thank you all.

There is one person whose help and guidance made this book possible. Jean Rysstad has been my North Star. It would not have happened without her. Sheila Peters and Lynn Shervill at Creekstone Press made it a reality. Without Bill's, Shirley's and Clint's encouragement and generosity, I might not have had the courage to complete the collection. My love and gratitude to you all is endless.

In all the years of Mom's and my expanding relationship, she only asked one thing of me. She asked me to make sure that both her names, Dorothy May, be engraved on her and Dad's headstone.

After her death, I made arrangements to have the headstone lifted and shipped to Vancouver for Mom's names and dates to be added. When the stone returned to Prince Rupert I bought flowers and went to the cemetery. I cannot express my shock and disappointment when I saw the stone. Engraved beneath Dad's name was:

1909 Dorothy M 2003

I was pleased that Mom and Dad were together again and tried to ignore the niggling that picked at my thoughts at quiet moments and walks in the woods on the many trails throughout Prince Rupert. It seemed that when I was alone, the image of the stone sprung to the forefront of my mind.

After a couple of months, I phoned Vince and told him that Mom only asked one thing of me and I felt I had let her down. I wanted her full name on the stone. Vince agreed that it should be done right and we made arrangements for the stone to be shipped back to Vancouver. Vince and Mike looked after the details from there. When the stone arrived back in Prince Rupert I bought more flowers and went back to the cemetery. Dorothy May was there with Holger Ole. Mom's request, and my promise to her, was fulfilled.

My daughter's third child is a girl, Allison May. Her mother is Shirley May. I am Shirley's mother, Nancy May. My mother was Dorothy May. Her mother was Florence May. The past knits its way through generations and continues its refrain; life carries on.